THE COMPLETE

SLOW COOKER

Cookbook for Beginners 2023

1600 Days of Nutritious and Simple Recipes to Simplify Your Cooking and Save Time in the Kitchen, Perfect for Busy Individuals and Families

Sebastian Duffy

CONTENTS

Vegetable & Vegetarian Recipes 31

Lunch & Dinner Recipes 38

Soups & Stews Recipes 45

Poultry Recipes 52

INTRODUCTION

Sebastian Duffy, a culinary artist known for his innovative approach to home cooking, has long been a proponent of techniques that combine simplicity, flavor, and mindfulness. In his latest creation, "Slow Cooker Cookbook," he delves into how to make a meal truly spiritually satisfying. Duffy's belief in slow cooking isn't just a method; it's a method. It's a culinary philosophy that embraces patience, quality and the joy of sharing experiences.

Born into a family of food lovers, Duffy began his journey into the culinary world at an early age. Inspired by the rich flavors from different cultures, he set out on a mission to demystify cooking, focusing on creating dishes that are both nutritious and delicious. With its humble appearance and its powerful ability to transform ingredients through gentle heat, the slow cooker was the perfect vehicle for Duffy to explore cooking.

This cookbook is a testament to Duffy's dedication to the craft of slow cooking. Here, he shares his wisdom and passion, taking you on a culinary adventure that goes beyond mere livelihood. These recipes will not only fill the stomach, but also nourish the soul. From tangy stews that evoke memories of family gatherings to delicate desserts that celebrate life's sweet moments, Duffy's slow cooker recipes celebrate food's ability to bring us together.

But Duffy's Cookbook is more than just a cookbook. This is a comprehensive guide that delves into the art and science of slow cooking. Whether you're an experienced home cook or just beginning your culinary journey, Duffy offers insights to help you deepen your understanding of this timeless method of cooking. He offers invaluable advice on choosing the right ingredients, explains the chemistry behind slow cooking, and provides guidance on how to create his signature dishes.

In embracing this cookbook, you not only adopt a new set of recipes, but you also embrace a culinary tradition that celebrates the simple joys of life.

What is Slow Cooker?

A slow cooker is a countertop electrical appliance designed to simmer food at a low temperature over several hours. Inside its outer shell, a heating element surrounds a removable ceramic or porcelain pot, distributing consistent and gentle heat to the ingredients placed within. Users can select different temperature settings, often categorized as "Low" or "High," to control the cooking time and intensity. The slow cooker's lid retains heat and moisture, allowing flavors to meld and tougher ingredients like meat to tenderize. Ideal for busy lifestyles, it offers a "set and forget" cooking method that transforms simple ingredients into rich and flavorful meals without the need for constant supervision.

What facilities can this Slow Cooker Cookbook provide?

Save time

Let the appliance do the work while you're on the go by offering recipes designed specifically for the slow cooker that allow you to prep meals ahead of time.

Variety

The cookbook is a collection of diverse recipes that break the monotony of everyday meals and introduce you to new dishes and flavors without professional cooking skills.

Easy to use

With clear instructions, handy tips, this cookbook simplifies the cooking process and makes it accessible to everyone.

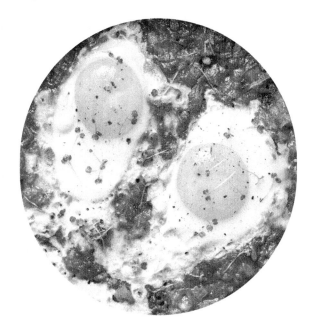

Healthy eating

Slow cooker recipes often emphasize whole, unprocessed ingredients. The cookbook guides you in creating nutritionally balanced meals to meet a variety of dietary needs and preferences.

Budget-friendly option

Slow cookers are known for creating delicious meals with less expensive cuts of meat and simple ingredients. The cookbook may include recipes that are on the budget without compromising on flavor.

Caters to different skill levels

Whether you're a beginner or an experienced cook, cookbooks may offer recipes of varying complexity, allowing you to grow and challenge yourself in the kitchen.

Explore Global Flavors

Several cookbooks expand culinary horizons by introducing readers to international dishes suitable for the slow cooker.

Seasonal and local ingredients guide

Guidance on how to use seasonal and local ingredients to create fresher, more sustainable dishes.

Some questions and answers about Slow Cooker

Can I put frozen meat in the slow cooker?

Putting frozen meat in a slow cooker is generally not recommended, as this may cause the meat to remain in the temperature "danger zone" for too long, increasing the risk of bacterial growth. Always defrost meat before putting it in the slow cooker.

Can I reheat leftovers in a slow cooker?

While it's possible to reheat leftovers in a slow cooker, it's not the most efficient way. Slow cookers heat food gradually, so it's usually best to reheat leftovers on the stovetop or in the microwave to ensure they reach a safe temperature quickly.

Can I cook pasta in a slow cooker?

Pasta can be cooked in a slow cooker, but timing is of the essence. Adding it too soon may result in the pasta being overcooked and mushy. It's usually best to add pasta towards the end of the cooking time, or cook it separately and add just before serving.

How Much Water Should I Use in a Slow Cooker?

Since the slow cooker retains most of the water, you generally need less water than with traditional stovetop cooking. In general, the water should just cover the main ingredients.

Is it safe to use a slow cooker overnight?

Many people use the slow cooker overnight to prepare breakfast dishes or stews without any issues. Be sure to follow safety guidelines and manufacturer instructions.

Some tips for your Slow Cooker

• **Preheat the slow cooker**

For best results, preheat the slow cooker about 20 minutes before adding ingredients, especially when cooking meat.

• **Layer wisely**

Place tougher, longer-cooking ingredients like root vegetables on the bottom so they receive more direct heat, and more delicate ingredients on top.

• **Avoid overfilling**

Most slow cookers work best when half to two-thirds full. Overfilling will result in uneven cooking.

• **Use the right cut of meat**

Tougher cuts of meat, such as roast shoulder, pork shoulder, or short ribs, usually work best because they break down and soften after prolonged cooking.

• **Dairy**

Dairy curdles after prolonged cooking, so add them towards the end of the cooking process if possible.

• **Avoid opening the lid**

Resist the temptation to check on food frequently, as opening the lid releases heat and can significantly increase cooking time.

- **Be careful with wine**

If your recipe calls for wine, be sure to boil off the alcohol first, as alcohol vapors can accumulate on the slow cooker lid and cause odors.

- **Use the correct size**

Match the recipe to the size of your slow cooker. Cooking small amounts of food in large pots or vice versa can affect cooking times and results.

- **Clean with care**

Avoid drastic temperature changes when cleaning to prevent cracking, especially with ceramic inserts.

Breakfast Recipes

Breakfast Recipes

Egg Bake

Servings: 8
Cooking Time: 8 Hours

Ingredients:
- 20 ounces tater tots
- 2 yellow onions, chopped
- 6 ounces bacon, chopped
- 2 cups cheddar cheese, shredded
- 12 eggs
- ¼ cup parmesan, grated
- 1 cup milk
- Salt and black pepper to the taste
- 4 tablespoons white flour
- Cooking spray

Directions:
1. Grease your Crock Pot with cooking spray and layer half of the tater tots, onions, bacon, cheddar and parmesan.
2. Continue layering the rest of the tater tots, bacon, onions, parmesan and cheddar.
3. In a bowl, mix the eggs with milk, salt, pepper and flour and whisk well.
4. Pour this into the Crock Pot, cover and cook on Low for 8 hours.
5. Slice, divide between plates and serve for breakfast.

Nutrition Info:
- Info calories 290, fat 9, fiber 1, carbs 9, protein 22

Bacon Muffins

Servings:5
Cooking Time: 4 Hours

Ingredients:
- ½ cup flour
- 2 tablespoons coconut oil
- 2 eggs, beaten
- 1 teaspoon baking powder
- 2 oz bacon, chopped, cooked
- ¼ cup milk

Directions:
1. Mix flour, milk, and eggs.
2. Add coconut oil, baking powder, and bacon. Stir the mixture carefully.
3. Then pour the batter in the muffin molds.
4. Transfer them in the Crock Pot and close the lid.
5. Cook the muffins on High for 4 hours.

Nutrition Info:
- InfoPer Serving: 186 calories, 8.1g protein, 10.9g carbohydrates, 12.3g fat, 0.4g fiber, 79mg cholesterol, 293mg sodium, 209mg potassium.

Breakfast Zucchini Oatmeal

Servings: 4
Cooking Time: 8 Hours

Ingredients:
- ½ cup steel cut oats
- 1 carrot, grated
- 1 and ½ cups coconut milk
- ¼ zucchini, grated
- A pinch of cloves, ground
- A pinch of nutmeg, ground
- ½ teaspoon cinnamon powder
- 2 tablespoons brown sugar
- ¼ cup pecans, chopped

Directions:
1. In your Crock Pot, mix oats with carrot, milk, zucchini, cloves, nutmeg, cinnamon and sugar, stir, cover and cook on Low for 8 hours.
2. Add pecans, toss, divide into bowls and serve.

Nutrition Info:
- Info calories 251, fat 6, fiber 8, carbs 19, protein 6

Maple Banana Oatmeal

Servings: 2
Cooking Time: 6 Hours

Ingredients:
- 1/2 cup old fashioned oats
- 1 banana, mashed
- ½ teaspoon cinnamon powder
- 2 tablespoons maple syrup
- 2 cups almond milk
- Cooking spray

Directions:
1. Grease your Crock Pot with the cooking spray, add the oats, banana and the other ingredients, stir, put the lid on and cook on Low for 6 hours.
2. Divide into 2 bowls and serve for breakfast.

Nutrition Info:
- Info calories 815, fat 60.3, fiber 10.7, carbs 67, protein 11.1

Strawberry Yogurt

Servings:7
Cooking Time: 3 Hours

Ingredients:
- 4 cup milk
- 1 cup Greek yogurt
- 1 cup strawberries, sliced
- 1 teaspoon coconut shred

Directions:
1. Pour the milk into the Crock Pot and cook it on HIGH for 3 hours.
2. Cool the milk till it reaches the temperature of 100F.
3. Add Greek yogurt, mix the liquid carefully, and cover with a towel.
4. Leave the yogurt for 10 hours in a warm place.
5. Pour the thick yogurt mixture in the colander or cheese mold and leave for 5 hours to avoid the extra liquid.
6. Transfer the cooked yogurt in the ramekins and top with sliced strawberries and coconut shred.

Nutrition Info:
- InfoPer Serving: 105 calories,7.6g protein, 9.9g carbohydrates, 4.2g fat, 0.6g fiber, 13mg cholesterol, 76mg sodium, 152mg potassium.

Chia Seeds And Chicken Breakfast

Servings: 4
Cooking Time: 3 Hours

Ingredients:
- 1 pound chicken breasts, skinless, boneless and cubed
- ½ teaspoon basil, dried
- ¾ cup flaxseed, ground
- ¼ cup chia seeds
- ¼ cup parmesan, grated
- ½ teaspoon oregano, chopped
- Salt and black pepper to the taste
- 2 eggs
- 2 garlic cloves, minced

Directions:
1. In a bowl, mix flaxseed with chia seeds, parmesan, salt, pepper, oregano, garlic and basil and stir.
2. Put the eggs in a second bowl and whisk them well.
3. Dip chicken in eggs mix, then in chia seeds mix, put them in your Crock Pot after you've greased it with cooking spray, cover and cook on High for 3 hours.
4. Serve them right away for a Sunday breakfast.

Nutrition Info:
- Info calories 212, fat 3, fiber 4, carbs 17, protein 4

Sweet Quinoa

Servings:4
Cooking Time: 3 Hours

Ingredients:
- 1 cup quinoa
- ¼ cup dates, chopped
- 3 cups of water
- 1 apricot, chopped
- ½ teaspoon ground nutmeg

Directions:
1. Put quinoa, dates, and apricot in the Crock Pot.
2. Add ground nutmeg and mix the mixture.
3. Cook it on high for 3 hours.

Nutrition Info:
- InfoPer Serving: 194 calories, 6.4g protein, 36.7g carbohydrates, 2.8g fat, 4.1g fiber, 0mg cholesterol, 8g sodium, 338mg potassium.

Lamb And Eggs Mix

Servings: 2
Cooking Time: 6 Hours

Ingredients:
- 1 pound lamb meat, ground
- 4 eggs, whisked
- 1 tablespoon basil, chopped
- ½ teaspoon cumin powder
- 1 tablespoon chili powder
- 1 red onion, chopped
- 1 tablespoon olive oil
- A pinch of salt and black pepper

Directions:
1. Grease the Crock Pot with the oil and mix the lamb with the eggs, basil and the other ingredients inside.
2. Toss, put the lid on, cook on Low for 6 hours, divide into bowls and serve for breakfast.

Nutrition Info:
- Info calories 220, fat 2, fiber 2, carbs 6, protein 2

Apple Crumble

Servings:2
Cooking Time: 5 Hours

Ingredients:
- 1 tablespoon liquid honey
- 2 Granny Smith apples
- 4 oz granola
- 4 tablespoons water
- 1 tablespoon almond butter
- 1 teaspoon vanilla extract

Directions:
1. Cut the apple into small wedges.
2. Remove the seeds from the apples and chop them into small pieces.
3. Put them in the Crock Pot.
4. Add water, almond butter, vanilla extract, and honey.
5. Cook the apples for 5 hours on Low.
6. Then stir them carefully.
7. Put the cooked apples and granola one-by-one in the serving glasses.

Nutrition Info:
- InfoPer Serving: 268 calories, 10.8g protein, 71.4g carbohydrates, 18.5g fat, 11.3g fiber, 0mg cholesterol, 17mg sodium, 613mg potassium.

Quinoa And Oats Mix

Servings: 6
Cooking Time: 7 Hours

Ingredients:
- ½ cup quinoa
- 1 and ½ cups steel cut oats
- 4 and ½ cups almond milk
- 2 tablespoons maple syrup
- 4 tablespoons brown sugar
- 1 and ½ teaspoons vanilla extract
- Cooking spray

Directions:
1. Grease your Crock Pot with cooking spray, add quinoa, oats, almond milk, maple syrup, sugar and vanilla extract, cover and cook on Low for 7 hours.
2. Stir, divide into bowls and serve for breakfast.

Nutrition Info:
- Info calories 251, fat 8, fiber 8, carbs 20, protein 5

Cheddar Eggs

Servings:4
Cooking Time: 2 Hours

Ingredients:
- 1 teaspoon butter, softened
- 4 eggs
- ½ teaspoon salt
- 1/3 cup Cheddar cheese, shredded

Directions:
1. Grease the Crock Pot bowl with butter and crack the eggs inside.
2. Sprinkle the eggs with salt and shredded cheese.
3. Close the lid and cook on High for 2 hours.

Nutrition Info:
- InfoPer Serving: 109 calories, 7.9g protein, 0.5g carbohydrates, 8.5g fat, 0g fiber, 176mg cholesterol, 418mg sodium, 69mg potassium.

Apple Oatmeal

Servings: 3
Cooking Time: 7 Hours 20 Minutes

Ingredients:
- ¼ cup brown sugar
- ¼ teaspoon salt
- 2 cups milk
- 2 tablespoons honey
- 2 tablespoons butter, melted
- ½ teaspoon cinnamon
- 1 cup apple, peeled and chopped
- ½ cup walnuts, chopped
- 1 cup steel cut oats
- ½ cup dates, chopped

Directions:
1. Grease a crock pot and add milk, honey, brown sugar, melted butter, cinnamon and salt.
2. Mix well and stir in the oats, apples, walnuts and dates.
3. Cover and cook on LOW for about 7 hours.
4. Dish out and stir well before serving.

Nutrition Info:
- Info Calories: 593 Fat: 25.3g Carbohydrates: 84.8g

Sweet Pepper Eggs

Servings:2
Cooking Time: 2.5 Hours

Ingredients:
- 1 sweet pepper
- 4 eggs
- ¼ teaspoon ground black pepper
- 1 teaspoon butter, melted

Directions:
1. Slice the sweet pepper into 4 rounds.
2. Then brush the Crock Pot with butter from inside.
3. Put the sweet pepper rounds in the Crock Pot in one layer.
4. Then crack the eggs in the sweet pepper rounds.
5. Sprinkle the eggs with ground black pepper and close the lid.
6. Cook the meal on High for 2.5 hours.

Nutrition Info:
- InfoPer Serving: 162 calories, 11.7g protein, 5.4g carbohydrates, 10.8g fat, 0.9g fiber, 332mg cholesterol, 138mg sodium, 234mg potassium.

Italian Style Scrambled Eggs

Servings:4
Cooking Time: 4 Hours

Ingredients:
- 4 eggs, beaten
- 3 oz Mozzarella, shredded
- ¼ cup milk
- 1 teaspoon Italian seasonings
- ¼ teaspoon salt
- 1 teaspoon butter, melted

Directions:
1. Mix eggs with milk, Italian seasonings, and salt.
2. Pour butter and milk mixture in the Crock Pot and close the lid.
3. Cook the meal on high for 1 hour.
4. Then open the lid and scramble the eggs.
5. After this, top the meal with cheese and cook the eggs on low for 3 hours more.

Nutrition Info:
- InfoPer Serving: 143 calories, 12.1g protein, 2g carbohydrates, 9.7g fat, 0g fiber, 180mg cholesterol, 351mg sodium, 69mg potassium.

Quinoa And Apricots

Servings: 6
Cooking Time: 10 Hours

Ingredients:
- ¾ cup quinoa
- ¾ cup steel cut oats
- 2 tablespoons honey
- 1 cup apricots, chopped
- 6 cups water
- 1 teaspoon vanilla extract
- ¾ cup hazelnuts, chopped

Directions:
1. In your Crock Pot, mix quinoa with oats honey, apricots, water, vanilla and hazelnuts, stir, cover and cook on Low for 10 hours.
2. Stir quinoa mix again, divide into bowls and serve for breakfast.

Nutrition Info:
- Info calories 200, fat 3, fiber 5, carbs 8, protein 6

Veggie Casserole

Servings: 8
Cooking Time: 4 Hours

Ingredients:
- 4 egg whites
- 8 eggs
- Salt and black pepper to the taste
- 2 teaspoons ground mustard
- ¾ cup milk
- 30 ounces hash browns
- 4 bacon strips, cooked and chopped
- 1 broccoli head, chopped
- 2 bell peppers, chopped
- Cooking spray
- 6 ounces cheddar cheese, shredded
- 1 small onion, chopped

Directions:
1. In a bowl, mix the egg white with eggs, salt, pepper, mustard and milk and whisk really well.
2. Grease your Crock Pot with the spray, add hash browns, broccoli, bell peppers and onion.
3. Pour eggs mix, sprinkle bacon and cheddar on top, cover and cook on Low for 4 hours.
4. Divide between plates and serve hot for breakfast.

Nutrition Info:
- Info calories 300, fat 4, fiber 8, carbs 18, protein 8

Basil Sausages

Servings:5
Cooking Time: 4 Hours

Ingredients:
- 1-pound Italian sausages, chopped
- 1 teaspoon dried basil
- 1 tablespoon olive oil
- 1 teaspoon ground coriander
- ¼ cup of water

Directions:
1. Sprinkle the chopped sausages with ground coriander and dried basil and transfer in the Crock Pot.
2. Add olive oil and water.
3. Close the lid and cook the sausages on high for 4 hours.

Nutrition Info:
- InfoPer Serving: 338 calories, 12.9g protein, 0.6g carbohydrates, 31.2g fat, 0g fiber, 69mg cholesterol, 664mg sodium, 231mg potassium.

Appetizers Recipes

Appetizers Recipes

Three Cheese Artichoke Sauce

Servings: 16
Cooking Time: 4 1/4 Hours

Ingredients:
- 1 jar artichoke hearts, drained and chopped
- 1 shallot, chopped
- 2 cups shredded mozzarella
- 1 cup grated Parmesan
- 1 cup grated Swiss cheese
- 1/2 teaspoon dried thyme
- 1/4 teaspoon chili powder

Directions:
1. Combine all the ingredients in your Crock Pot.
2. Cover the pot with its lid and cook on low setting for 4 hours.
3. The sauce is great served warm with vegetable sticks or biscuits or even small pretzels.

Artichoke Dip

Servings: 20
Cooking Time: 6 1/4 Hours

Ingredients:
- 2 sweet onions, chopped
- 1 red chili, chopped
- 2 garlic cloves, chopped
- 1 jar artichoke hearts, drained and chopped
- 1 cup cream cheese
- 1 cup heavy cream
- 2 oz. blue cheese, crumbled
- 2 tablespoons chopped cilantro

Directions:
1. Mix the onions, chili, garlic, artichoke hearts, cream cheese, heavy cream and blue cheese in a Crock Pot.
2. Cook on low settings for 6 hours.
3. When done, stir in the cilantro and serve the dip warm or chilled.

Sausage And Pepper Appetizer

Servings: 8
Cooking Time: 6 1/4 Hours

Ingredients:
- 6 fresh pork sausages, skins removed
- 2 tablespoons olive oil
- 1 can fire roasted tomatoes
- 4 roasted bell peppers, chopped
- 1 poblano pepper, chopped
- 1 shallot, chopped
- 1 cup grated Provolone cheese
- Salt and pepper to taste

Directions:
1. Heat the oil in a skillet and stir in the sausage meat. Cook for 5 minutes, stirring often.
2. Transfer the meat in your Crock Pot and add the remaining ingredients.
3. Season with salt and pepper and cook on low settings for 6 hours.
4. Serve the dish warm or chilled.

Bacon Wrapped Dates

Servings: 8
Cooking Time: 1 3/4 Hours

Ingredients:
- 16 dates, pitted
- 16 almonds
- 16 slices bacon

Directions:
1. Stuff each date with an almond.
2. Wrap each date in bacon and place the wrapped dates in your Crock Pot.
3. Cover with its lid and cook on high settings for 1 1/4 hours.
4. Serve warm or chilled.

Molasses Lime Meatballs

Servings: 10
Cooking Time: 8 1/4 Hours

Ingredients:
- 3 pounds ground beef
- 2 garlic cloves, minced
- 1 shallot, chopped
- 1/2 cup oat flour
- 1/2 teaspoon cumin powder
- 1/2 teaspoon chili powder
- 1 egg
- Salt and pepper to taste
- 1/2 cup molasses
- 1/4 cup soy sauce
- 2 tablespoons lime juice
- 1/2 cup beef stock
- 1 tablespoon Worcestershire sauce

Directions:
1. Combine the molasses, soy sauce, lime juice, stock and Worcestershire sauce in your Crock Pot.
2. In a bowl, mix the ground beef, garlic, shallot, oat flour, cumin powder, chili powder, egg, salt and pepper and mix well.
3. Form small balls and place them in the sauce.
4. Cover the pot and cook on low settings for 8 hours.
5. Serve the meatballs warm or chilled.

Green Vegetable Dip

Servings: 12
Cooking Time: 2 1/4 Hours

Ingredients:
- 10 oz. frozen spinach, thawed and drained
- 1 jar artichoke hearts, drained
- 1 cup chopped parsley
- 1 cup cream cheese
- 1 cup sour cream
- 1/2 cup grated Parmesan cheese
- 1/2 cup feta cheese, crumbled
- 1/2 teaspoon onion powder
- 1/4 teaspoon garlic powder

Directions:
1. Combine all the ingredients in your Crock Pot and mix gently.
2. Cover with its lid and cook on high settings for 2 hours.
3. Serve the dip warm or chilled with crusty bread, biscuits or other salty snacks or even vegetable sticks.

Goat Cheese Stuffed Mushrooms

Servings: 6
Cooking Time: 4 1/4 Hours

Ingredients:
- 12 medium size mushrooms
- 6 oz. goat cheese
- 1 egg
- 1/2 cup breadcrumbs
- 1 poblano pepper, chopped
- 1 teaspoon dried oregano

Directions:
1. Mix the goat cheese, egg, breadcrumbs, pepper and oregano in a bowl.
2. Stuff each mushroom with the goat cheese mixture and place them all in a Crock Pot.
3. Cover the pot and cook on low settings for 4 hours.
4. Serve the mushrooms warm or chilled.

White Bean Hummus

Servings: 8
Cooking Time: 8 1/4 Hours

Ingredients:
- 1 pound dried white beans, rinsed
- 2 cups water
- 2 cups chicken stock
- 1 bay leaf
- 1 thyme sprig
- 4 garlic cloves, minced
- Salt and pepper to taste
- 2 tablespoons canola oil
- 2 large sweet onions, sliced

Directions:
1. Combine the white beans, water, stock, bay leaf and thyme in your Crock Pot.
2. Add salt and pepper to taste and cook the beans on low settings for 8 hours.
3. When done, drain the beans well (but reserve 1/4 cup of the liquid) and discard the bay leaf and thyme.
4. Transfer the bean in a food processor. Add the reserved liquid and pulse until smooth.
5. Season with salt and pepper and transfer in a bowl.
6. Heat the canola oil in a skillet and add the onions. Cook for 10 minutes over medium flame until the onions begin to caramelize.
7. Top the hummus with caramelized onions and serve.

Queso Verde Dip

Servings: 12
Cooking Time: 4 1/4 Hours

Ingredients:
- 1 pound ground chicken
- 2 shallots, chopped
- 2 tablespoons olive oil
- 2 cups salsa verde
- 1 cup cream cheese
- 2 cups grated Cheddar
- 2 poblano peppers, chopped
- 1 tablespoon Worcestershire sauce
- 4 garlic cloves, minced
- 1/4 cup chopped cilantro
- Salt and pepper to taste

Directions:
1. Combine all the ingredients in your Crock Pot.
2. Add salt and pepper to taste and cook on low heat for 4 hours.
3. The dip is best served warm.

Sausage Dip

Servings: 8
Cooking Time: 6 1/4 Hours

Ingredients:
- 1 pound fresh pork sausages
- 1 pound spicy pork sausages
- 1 cup cream cheese
- 1 can diced tomatoes
- 2 poblano peppers, chopped

Directions:
1. Combine all the ingredients in a crock pot.
2. Cook on low settings for 6 hours.
3. Serve warm or chilled.

Honey Glazed Chicken Drumsticks

Servings: 8
Cooking Time: 7 1/4 Hours

Ingredients:
- 3 pounds chicken drumsticks
- 1/4 cup soy sauce
- 1/4 cup honey
- 1 teaspoon rice vinegar
- 1/2 teaspoon sesame oil
- 2 tablespoons tomato paste
- 1/2 teaspoon dried Thai basil

Directions:
1. Combine all the ingredients in your Crock Pot and toss them around until the drumsticks are evenly coated.
2. Cover the pot with its lid and cook on low settings for 7 hours.
3. Serve the chicken drumsticks warm or chilled.

Pepperoni Pizza Dip

Servings: 10
Cooking Time: 3 1/4 Hours

Ingredients:
- 1 1/2 cups pizza sauce
- 4 peperoni, sliced
- 2 shallots, chopped
- 2 red bell peppers, diced
- 1/2 cup black olives, pitted and chopped
- 1 cup cream cheese
- 1 cup shredded mozzarella
- 1/2 teaspoon dried basil

Directions:
1. Combine the pizza sauce and the rest of the ingredients in your Crock Pot.
2. Cover the pot with its lid and cook on low settings for 3 hours.
3. The dip is best served warm with bread sticks or tortilla chips.

Teriyaki Chicken Wings

Servings: 6
Cooking Time: 6 1/4 Hours

Ingredients:
- 2 tablespoons brown sugar
- 1 tablespoon molasses
- 1/2 teaspoon garlic powder
- 1/2 teaspoon ground ginger
- 1/2 cup soy sauce
- 1/2 cup pineapple juice
- 1/4 cup water
- 2 tablespoons canola oil
- 3 pounds chicken wings

Directions:
1. Combine all the ingredients in a Crock Pot and mix until evenly coated.
2. Cover the pot with its lid and cook on low settings for 6 hours.
3. Serve the chicken wings warm or chilled.

Candied Kielbasa

Servings: 8
Cooking Time: 6 1/4 Hours

Ingredients:
- 2 pounds kielbasa sausages
- 1/2 cup brown sugar
- 1 cup BBQ sauce
- 1 teaspoon prepared horseradish
- 1/2 teaspoon black pepper
- 1/4 teaspoon cumin powder

Directions:
1. Combine all the ingredients in a Crock Pot, adding salt if needed.
2. Cook on low settings for 6 hours.
3. Serve the kielbasa warm or chilled.

Bacon Chicken Sliders

Servings: 8
Cooking Time: 4 1/2 Hours

Ingredients:
- 2 pounds ground chicken
- 1 egg
- 1/2 cup breadcrumbs
- 1 shallot, chopped
- Salt and pepper to taste
- 8 bacon slices

Directions:
1. Mix the chicken, egg, breadcrumbs and shallot in a bowl. Add salt and pepper to taste and give it a good mix.
2. Form small sliders then wrap each slider in a bacon slice.
3. Place the sliders in a Crock Pot.
4. Cover with its lid and cook on high settings for 4 hours, making sure to flip them over once during cooking.
5. Serve them warm.

Ham And Swiss Cheese Dip

Servings: 6
Cooking Time: 4 1/4 Hours

Ingredients:
- 1 pound ham, diced
- 1 cup cream cheese
- 1 can condensed cream of mushroom soup
- 1 can condensed onion soup
- 2 cups grated Swiss cheese
- 1/2 teaspoon chili powder

Directions:
1. Combine all the ingredients in a Crock Pot.
2. Cook on low settings for 4 hours.
3. Serve the dip preferably warm.

Cheese And Beer Fondue

Servings: 10
Cooking Time: 2 1/4 Hours

Ingredients:
- 4 tablespoons butter
- 1 shallot, chopped
- 2 garlic cloves, minced
- 2 tablespoons all-purpose flour
- 2 poblano peppers, chopped
- 1 cup milk
- 1 cup light beer
- 2 cups grated Cheddar
- 1/2 teaspoon chili powder

Directions:
1. Melt the butter in a saucepan and stir in the shallot and garlic. Sauté for 2 minutes then add the flour and cook for 2 additional minutes.
2. Stir in the milk and cook until thickened, about 5 minutes.
3. Pour the mixture in your Crock Pot and stir in the remaining ingredients.
4. Cook on high settings for 2 hours and serve the fondue warm with biscuits or other salty snacks.

Side Dish Recipes

Side Dish Recipes

Eggplant And Kale Mix

Servings: 6
Cooking Time: 2 Hours

Ingredients:
- 14 ounces canned roasted tomatoes and garlic
- 4 cups eggplant, cubed
- 1 yellow bell pepper, chopped
- 1 red onion, cut into medium wedges
- 4 cups kale leaves
- 2 tablespoons olive oil
- 1 teaspoon mustard
- 3 tablespoons red vinegar
- 1 garlic clove, minced
- Salt and black pepper to the taste
- ½ cup basil, chopped

Directions:
1. In your Crock Pot, mix the eggplant with tomatoes, bell pepper and onion, toss, cover and cook on High for 2 hours.
2. Add kale, toss, cover Crock Pot and leave aside for now.
3. In a bowl, mix oil with vinegar, mustard, garlic, salt and pepper and whisk well.
4. Add this over eggplant mix, also add basil, toss, divide between plates and serve as a side dish.

Nutrition Info:
- Info calories 251, fat 9, fiber 6, carbs 34, protein 8

Lemon Kale Mix

Servings: 2
Cooking Time: 2 Hours

Ingredients:
- 1 yellow bell pepper, chopped
- 1 red bell pepper, chopped
- 1 tablespoon olive oil
- 1 red onion, sliced
- 4 cups baby kale
- 1 teaspoon lemon zest, grated
- 1 tablespoon lemon juice
- ½ cup veggie stock
- 1 garlic clove, minced
- A pinch of salt and black pepper
- 1 tablespoon basil, chopped

Directions:
1. In your Crock Pot, mix the kale with the oil, onion, bell peppers and the other ingredients, toss, put the lid on and cook on Low for 2 hours.
2. Divide the mix between plates and serve as a side dish.

Nutrition Info:
- Info calories 251, fat 9, fiber 6, carbs 7, protein 8

Curry Broccoli Mix

Servings: 2
Cooking Time: 3 Hours

Ingredients:
- 1 pound broccoli florets
- 1 cup tomato paste
- 1 tablespoon red curry paste
- 1 red onion, sliced
- ½ teaspoon Italian seasoning
- 1 teaspoon thyme, dried
- Salt and black pepper to the taste
- ½ tablespoon cilantro, chopped

Directions:
1. In your Crock Pot, mix the broccoli with the curry paste, tomato paste and the other ingredients, toss, put the lid on and cook on Low for 3 hours.
2. Divide the mix between plates and serve as a side dish.

Nutrition Info:
- Info calories 177, fat 12, fiber 2, carbs 7, protein 7

Herbed Balsamic Beets

Servings: 4
Cooking Time: 7 Hours

Ingredients:
- 6 medium assorted-color beets, peeled and cut into wedges
- 2 tbsp balsamic vinegar
- 2 tbsp olive oil
- 2 tbsp chives, chopped
- 1 tbsp tarragon, chopped
- Salt and black pepper to the taste
- 1 tsp orange peel, grated

Directions:
1. Add beets, tarragon, and rest of the ingredients to the Crock Pot.
2. Put the cooker's lid on and set the cooking time to 7 hours on Low settings.
3. Serve warm.

Nutrition Info:
- Info Per Serving: Calories: 144, Total Fat: 3g, Fiber: 1g, Total Carbs: 17g, Protein: 3g

Turmeric Buckwheat

Servings: 6
Cooking Time: 4 Hrs

Ingredients:
- 4 tbsp milk powder
- 2 tbsp butter
- 1 carrot
- 4 cup buckwheat
- 4 cups chicken stock
- 1 tbsp salt
- 1 tbsp turmeric
- 1 tsp paprika

Directions:
1. Whisk milk powder with buckwheat, stock, salt, turmeric, and paprika in the Crock Pot.
2. Stir in carrot strips and mix gently.
3. Put the cooker's lid on and set the cooking time to 4 hours on High settings.
4. Stir in butter then serve warm.

Nutrition Info:
- Info Per Serving: Calories: 238, Total Fat: 6.6g, Fiber: 4g, Total Carbs: 37.85g, Protein: 9g

Maple Brussels Sprouts

Servings: 12
Cooking Time: 3 Hours

Ingredients:
- 1 cup red onion, chopped
- 2 pounds Brussels sprouts, trimmed and halved
- Salt and black pepper to the taste
- ¼ cup apple juice
- 3 tablespoons olive oil
- ¼ cup maple syrup
- 1 tablespoon thyme, chopped

Directions:

1. In your Crock Pot, mix Brussels sprouts with onion, salt, pepper and apple juice, toss, cover and cook on Low for 3 hours.
2. In a bowl, mix maple syrup with oil and thyme, whisk really well, add over Brussels sprouts, toss well, divide between plates and serve as a side dish.

Nutrition Info:
- Info calories 100, fat 4, fiber 4, carbs 14, protein 3

Apples And Potatoes

Servings: 10
Cooking Time: 7 Hours

Ingredients:
- 2 green apples, cored and cut into wedges
- 3 pounds sweet potatoes, peeled and cut into medium wedges
- 1 cup coconut cream
- ½ cup dried cherries
- 1 cup apple butter
- 1 and ½ teaspoon pumpkin pie spice

Directions:

1. In your Crock Pot, mix sweet potatoes with green apples, cream, cherries, apple butter and spice, toss, cover and cook on Low for 7 hours.
2. Toss, divide between plates and serve as a side dish.

Nutrition Info:
- Info calories 351, fat 8, fiber 5, carbs 48, protein 2

Butternut Squash And Eggplant Mix

Servings: 2
Cooking Time: 4 Hours

Ingredients:
- 1 butternut squash, peeled and roughly cubed
- 1 eggplant, roughly cubed
- 1 red onion, chopped
- Cooking spray
- ½ cup veggie stock
- ¼ cup tomato paste
- ½ tablespoon parsley, chopped
- Salt and black pepper to the taste
- 2 garlic cloves, minced

Directions:

1. Grease the Crock Pot with the cooking spray and mix the squash with the eggplant, onion and the other ingredients inside.
2. Put the lid on and cook on Low for 4 hours.
3. Divide between plates and serve as a side dish.

Nutrition Info:
- Info calories 114, fat 4, fiber 4, carbs 18, protein 4

Refried Black Beans

Servings: 10
Cooking Time: 9 Hours

Ingredients:
- 5 oz. white onion, peeled and chopped
- 4 cups black beans
- 1 chili pepper, chopped
- 1 oz. minced garlic
- 10 cups water
- 1 tsp salt
- ½ tsp ground black pepper
- ¼ tsp cilantro, chopped

Directions:
1. Add onion, black beans and all other ingredients to the Crock Pot.
2. Put the cooker's lid on and set the cooking time to 9 hours on Low settings.
3. Strain all the excess liquid out of the beans while leaving only ¼ cup of the liquid.
4. Transfer the beans-onion mixture to a food processor and blend until smooth.
5. Serve fresh.

Nutrition Info:
- Info Per Serving: Calories: 73, Total Fat: 1.5g, Fiber: 4g, Total Carbs: 12.34g, Protein: 3g

Cauliflower And Carrot Gratin

Servings: 12
Cooking Time: 7 Hours

Ingredients:
- 16 ounces baby carrots
- 6 tablespoons butter, soft
- 1 cauliflower head, florets separated
- Salt and black pepper to the taste
- 1 yellow onion, chopped
- 1 teaspoon mustard powder
- 1 and ½ cups milk
- 6 ounces cheddar cheese, grated
- ½ cup breadcrumbs

Directions:
1. Put the butter in your Crock Pot, add carrots, cauliflower, onion, salt, pepper, mustard powder and milk and toss.
2. Sprinkle cheese and breadcrumbs all over, cover and cook on Low for 7 hours.
3. Divide between plates and serve as a side dish.

Nutrition Info:
- Info calories 182, fat 4, fiber 7, carbs 9, protein 4

Garlic Butter Green Beans

Servings: 6
Cooking Time: 2 Hours

Ingredients:
- 22 ounces green beans
- 2 garlic cloves, minced
- ¼ cup butter, soft
- 2 tablespoons parmesan, grated

Directions:
1. In your Crock Pot, mix green beans with garlic, butter and parmesan, toss, cover and cook on High for 2 hours.
2. Divide between plates, sprinkle parmesan all over and serve as a side dish.

Nutrition Info:
- Info calories 60, fat 4, fiber 1, carbs 3, protein 1

Lemony Honey Beets

Servings: 6
Cooking Time: 8 Hrs

Ingredients:

- 6 beets, peeled and cut into medium wedges
- 2 tbsp honey
- 2 tbsp olive oil
- 2 tbsp lemon juice
- Salt and black pepper to the taste
- 1 tbsp white vinegar
- ½ tsp lemon peel, grated

Directions:

1. Add beets, honey, oil, salt, black pepper, lemon peel, vinegar, and lemon juice to the Crock Pot.
2. Put the cooker's lid on and set the cooking time to 8 hours on Low settings.
3. Serve warm.

Nutrition Info:

- Info Per Serving: Calories: 80, Total Fat: 3g, Fiber: 4g, Total Carbs: 8g, Protein: 4g

Cheddar Potatoes Mix

Servings: 2
Cooking Time: 3 Hours

Ingredients:

- ½ pound gold potatoes, peeled and cut into wedges
- 2 ounces heavy cream
- ½ teaspoon turmeric powder
- ½ teaspoon rosemary, dried
- ¼ cup cheddar cheese, shredded
- 1 tablespoon butter, melted
- Cooking spray
- A pinch of salt and black pepper

Directions:

1. Grease your Crock Pot with the cooking spray, add the potatoes, cream, turmeric and the other ingredients, toss, put the lid on and cook on High for 3 hours.
2. Divide between plates and serve as a side dish.

Nutrition Info:

- Info calories 300, fat 14, fiber 6, carbs 22, protein 6

Mustard Brussels Sprouts

Servings: 2
Cooking Time: 3 Hours

Ingredients:

- 1 pound Brussels sprouts, trimmed and halved
- 1 tablespoon olive oil
- 1 tablespoon mustard
- 1 tablespoon balsamic vinegar
- Salt and black pepper to the taste
- ¼ cup veggie stock
- A pinch of red pepper, crushed
- 2 tablespoons chives, chopped

Directions:

1. In your Crock Pot, mix the Brussels sprouts with the oil, mustard and the other ingredients, toss, put the lid on and cook on High for 3 hours.
2. Divide the mix between plates and serve as a side dish.

Nutrition Info:

- Info calories 256, fat 12, fiber 6, carbs 8, protein 15

Broccoli Mix

Servings: 10
Cooking Time: 2 Hours

Ingredients:
- 6 cups broccoli florets
- 1 and ½ cups cheddar cheese, shredded
- 10 ounces canned cream of celery soup
- ½ teaspoon Worcestershire sauce
- ¼ cup yellow onion, chopped
- Salt and black pepper to the taste
- 1 cup crackers, crushed
- 2 tablespoons soft butter

Directions:
1. In a bowl, mix broccoli with cream of celery soup, cheese, salt, pepper, onion and Worcestershire sauce, toss and transfer to your Crock Pot.
2. Add butter, toss again, sprinkle crackers, cover and cook on High for 2 hours.
3. Serve as a side dish.

Nutrition Info:
- Info calories 159, fat 11, fiber 1, carbs 11, protein 6

Potatoes And Leeks Mix

Servings: 2
Cooking Time: 4 Hours

Ingredients:
- 2 leeks, sliced
- ½ pound sweet potatoes, cut into medium wedges
- ½ cup veggie stock
- ½ tablespoon balsamic vinegar
- 1 tablespoon chives, chopped
- ½ teaspoon pumpkin pie spice

Directions:
1. In your Crock Pot, mix the leeks with the potatoes and the other ingredients, toss, put the lid on and cook on High for 4 hours.
2. Divide between plates and serve as a side dish.

Nutrition Info:
- Info calories 351, fat 8, fiber 5, carbs 48, protein 7

Hot Zucchini Mix

Servings: 2
Cooking Time: 2 Hours

Ingredients:
- ¼ cup carrots, grated
- 1 pound zucchinis, roughly cubed
- 1 teaspoon hot paprika
- ½ teaspoon chili powder
- 2 spring onions, chopped
- ½ tablespoon olive oil
- ½ teaspoon curry powder
- 1 garlic clove, minced
- ½ teaspoon ginger powder
- A pinch of salt and black pepper
- 1 tablespoon cilantro, chopped

Directions:
1. In your Crock Pot, mix the carrots with the zucchinis, paprika and the other ingredients, toss, put the lid on and cook on Low for 2 hours.
2. Divide between plates and serve as a side dish.

Nutrition Info:
- Info calories 200, fat 5, fiber 7, carbs 28, protein 4

Vegetable & Vegetarian Recipes

Vegetable & Vegetarian Recipes

Wild Rice Peppers

Servings: 5
Cooking Time: 7.5 Hrs

Ingredients:
- 1 tomato, chopped
- 1 cup wild rice, cooked
- 4 oz. ground chicken
- 2 oz. mushroom, sliced
- ½ onion, sliced
- 1 tsp salt
- 1 tsp turmeric
- 1 tsp curry powder
- 1 cup chicken stock
- 2 tsp tomato paste
- 1 oz. black olives
- 5 red sweet pepper, cut the top off and seeds removed

Directions:
1. Toss rice with salt, turmeric, olives, tomato, onion, chicken, mushrooms, curry powder in a bowl.
2. Pour tomato paste and chicken stock into the Crock Pot.
3. Stuff the sweet peppers with chicken mixture.
4. Place the stuffed peppers in the cooker.
5. Put the cooker's lid on and set the cooking time to 7 hours 30 minutes on Low settings.
6. Serve warm with tomato gravy.

Nutrition Info:
- Info Per Serving: Calories 232, Total Fat 3.7g, Fiber 5g, Total Carbs 41.11g, Protein 12g

Mushroom Bourguignon

Servings:3
Cooking Time: 7 Hours

Ingredients:
- ½ cup mushrooms, chopped
- ¼ cup onion, chopped
- ¼ cup carrot, diced
- ½ cup green peas, frozen
- 1 teaspoon dried thyme
- 1 teaspoon salt
- 2 tablespoons tomato paste
- 3 cups vegetable stock

Directions:
1. Mix vegetable stock with tomato paste and pour liquid in the Crock Pot.
2. Add all remaining ingredients and close the lid.
3. Cook the meal on Low for 7 hours.

Nutrition Info:
- InfoPer Serving: 45 calories, 2.8g protein, 8.8g carbohydrates, 0.3g fat, 2.9g fiber, 0mg cholesterol, 844mg sodium, 250mg potassium.

Crockpot Baked Tofu

Servings:4
Cooking Time: 2 Hours

Ingredients:
- 1 small package extra firm tofu, sliced
- 3 tablespoons soy sauce
- 1 tablespoon sesame oil
- 2 teaspoons minced garlic
- Juice from ½ lemon, freshly squeezed

Directions:
1. In a deep dish, mix together the soy sauce, sesame oil, garlic, and lemon. Add a few tablespoons of water if the sauce is too thick.
2. Marinate the tofu slices for at least 2 hours.
3. Line the crockpot with foil and grease it with cooking spray.
4. Place the slices of marinated tofu into the crockpot.
5. Cook on low for 4 hours or on high for 2 hours.
6. Make sure that the tofu slices have a crispy outer texture.

Nutrition Info:
- Info Calories per serving:145; Carbohydrates: 4.1g; Protein: 11.6g; Fat: 10.8g; Sugar: 0.6g; Sodium: 142mg; Fiber:1.5 g

Cashew And Tofu Casserole

Servings:4
Cooking Time: 3.5 Hours

Ingredients:
- 1 oz cashews, crushed
- 6 oz firm tofu, chopped
- 1 cup broccoli, chopped
- 1 red onion, sliced
- 1 tablespoon avocado oil
- ¼ cup of soy sauce
- ¼ cup maple syrup
- 1 tablespoon cornstarch
- ½ cup of water
- 1 teaspoon garlic powder

Directions:
1. Pour the avocado oil in the Crock Pot.
2. Then sprinkle the broccoli with garlic powder and put it in the Crock Pot.

3. Add cornstarch.
4. After this, add maple syrup, soy sauce, onion, and tofu.
5. Add cashews and water.
6. Close the lid and cook the casserole on Low for 3.5 hours.

Nutrition Info:
- InfoPer Serving: 164 calories, 6.7g protein, 24g carbohydrates, 5.7g fat, 2.1g fiber, 0mg cholesterol, 917mg sodium, 309mg potassium.

Braised Swiss Chard

Servings:4
Cooking Time: 30 Minutes

Ingredients:
- 1-pound swiss chard, chopped
- 1 lemon
- 1 teaspoon garlic, diced
- 1 tablespoon sunflower oil
- 1 teaspoon salt
- 2 cups of water

Directions:
1. Put the swiss chard in the Crock Pot.
2. Cut the lemon into halves and squeeze it over the swiss chard.
3. After this, sprinkle the greens with diced garlic, sunflower oil, salt, and water.
4. Mix the mixture gently with the help of the spoon and close the lid.
5. Cook the greens on High for 30 minutes.

Nutrition Info:
- InfoPer Serving: 58 calories, 2.2g protein, 5.8g carbohydrates, 3.9g fat, 2.3g fiber, 0mg cholesterol, 828mg sodium, 455mg potassium.

Pumpkin Bean Chili

Servings: 6
Cooking Time: 5 Hrs

Ingredients:

- 1 cup pumpkin puree
- 30 oz. canned kidney beans, drained
- 30 oz. canned roasted tomatoes, chopped
- 2 cups of water
- 1 cup red lentils, dried
- 1 cup yellow onion, chopped
- 1 jalapeno pepper, chopped
- 1 tbsp chili powder
- 1 tbsp cocoa powder
- ½ tsp cinnamon powder
- 2 tsp cumin, ground
- A pinch of cloves, ground
- Salt and black pepper to the taste
- 2 tomatoes, chopped

Directions:

1. Add pumpkin puree along with other ingredients except for tomatoes, to the Crock Pot.
2. Put the cooker's lid on and set the cooking time to 5 hours on High settings.
3. Serve with tomatoes on top.
4. Enjoy.

Nutrition Info:

- Info Per Serving: Calories 266, Total Fat 6g, Fiber 4g, Total Carbs 12g, Protein 4g

Sweet Potato Curry

Servings:4
Cooking Time: 3.5 Hours

Ingredients:

- 2 cups sweet potatoes, chopped
- 1 cup spinach, chopped
- ½ onion, diced
- 1 teaspoon garlic, minced
- 1 teaspoon curry powder
- ½ teaspoon ground turmeric
- 1 tablespoon coconut oil
- 1 cup of coconut milk

Directions:

1. In the mixing bowl mix coconut milk, ground turmeric, curry powder, garlic, and pour it in the Crock Pot.
2. Add sweet potatoes, onion, and coconut oil.
3. Close the lid and cook the ingredients on High for 3 hours.
4. Then add spinach, carefully mix the mixture and cook it for 30 minutes on High.

Nutrition Info:

- InfoPer Serving: 267 calories, 3g protein, 26.5g carbohydrates, 18g fat, 5.1g fiber, 0mg cholesterol, 23mg sodium, 849mg potassium.

Hot Tofu

Servings:4
Cooking Time: 4 Hours

Ingredients:

- 1-pound firm tofu, cubed
- 1 tablespoon hot sauce
- ½ cup vegetable stock
- 1 teaspoon miso paste

Directions:

1. Mix vegetables tock with miso paste and pour in the Crock Pot.
2. Add hot sauce and tofu.
3. Close the lid and cook the meal on Low for 4 hours.
4. Then transfer the tofu and liquid in the serving bowls.

Nutrition Info:

- InfoPer Serving: 83 calories, 9.5g protein, 2.5g carbohydrates, 4.8g fat, 1.2g fiber, 0mg cholesterol, 168mg sodium, 176mg potassium.

Mung Beans Salad

Servings:4
Cooking Time: 3 Hours

Ingredients:
- ½ avocado, chopped
- 1 cup cherry tomatoes, halved
- ½ cup corn kernels, cooked
- 1 cup mung beans
- 3 cups of water
- 1 tablespoon lemon juice
- 1 tablespoon avocado oil

Directions:
1. Put mung beans in the Crock Pot.
2. Add water and cook them on High for 3 hours.
3. Then drain water and transfer the mung beans in the salad bowl.
4. Add avocado, cherry tomatoes, corn kernels, and shake well.
5. Then sprinkle the salad with avocado oil and lemon juice.

Nutrition Info:
- InfoPer Serving: 287 calories, 13.9g protein, 40g carbohydrates, 9.4g fat, 11.2g fiber, 0mg cholesterol, 20mg sodium, 932mg potassium.

Oregano Cheese Pie

Servings: 6
Cooking Time: 3.5 Hrs

Ingredients:
- 1 tsp baking soda
- 1 tbsp lemon juice
- 1 cup flour
- 1 cup milk
- 1 tsp salt
- 5 oz. Cheddar cheese, shredded
- 5 oz. Parmesan cheese, shredded
- 2 eggs
- ½ tsp oregano
- 1/3 tsp olive oil

Directions:
1. Sift flour with salt, oregano, baking soda and shredded cheese in a bowl.
2. Beat eggs with lemon juice and milk in a separate bowl.
3. Gradually stir in flour mixture and mix using a hand mixer until it forms a smooth dough.
4. Layer the base of Crock Pot with olive oil and spread the dough in the cooker.
5. Put the cooker's lid on and set the cooking time to 3 hours 30 minutes on High settings.
6. Serve.

Nutrition Info:
- Info Per Serving: Calories 288, Total Fat 13.7g, Fiber 1g, Total Carbs 24.23g, Protein 16g

Carrot And Lentils Sauté

Servings:4
Cooking Time: 5 Hours

Ingredients:
- 1 cup red lentils
- 1 cup carrot, diced
- 1 cup fresh parsley, chopped
- 4 cups vegetable stock
- 1 teaspoon cayenne pepper
- 1 teaspoon salt
- 1 tablespoon tomato paste

Directions:
1. Put all ingredients in the Crock Pot and gently stir.
2. Close the lid and cook the meal on low for 5 hours.

Nutrition Info:
- InfoPer Serving: 201 calories, 13.3g protein, 35.5g carbohydrates, 2.7g fat, 16.1g fiber, 0mg cholesterol, 1336mg sodium, 679mg potassium.

Crockpot Cumin-roasted Vegetables

Servings:2
Cooking Time:4 Hours

Ingredients:

- 1 red bell pepper, chopped
- 1 yellow bell pepper, chopped
- 1 green bell pepper, chopped
- ½ cup cherry tomatoes
- ¼ cup pepita seeds
- 6 cups kale leaves, chopped
- 4 tablespoon olive oil
- 1 teaspoon cumin
- 1 teaspoon dried oregano
- ¼ teaspoon salt

Directions:

1. Place all ingredients in a mixing bowl. Toss to coat everything with oil.
2. Line the bottom of the CrockPot with foil.
3. Place the vegetables inside.
4. Close the lid and cook on low for 4 hours or on high for 6 hours until the vegetables are a bit brown on the edges.

Nutrition Info:

- Info Calories per serving:380; Carbohydrates: 13.8g; Protein: 8.6g; Fat:35.8g; Sugar:1.7 g; Sodium: 512mg; Fiber: 6.6g

Curried Vegetable Stew

Servings:10
Cooking Time: 3 Hours

Ingredients:

- 1 teaspoon olive oil
- 1 onion, diced
- 2 tablespoon curry powder
- 1 tablespoon grated ginger
- 3 cloves of garlic, minced
- 1/8 teaspoon cayenne pepper
- 1 cup tomatoes, crushed
- 1 bag baby spinach
- 1 yellow bell pepper, chopped
- 1 red bell pepper, chopped
- 2 cups vegetable broth

- 1 cup coconut milk
- Salt and pepper to taste

Directions:

1. Place all ingredients in the CrockPot.
2. Give a good stir.
3. Close the lid and cook on high for 2 hours or on low for 3 hours.

Nutrition Info:

- Info Calories per serving: 88; Carbohydrates: 5.1g; Protein: 2.9g; Fat: 9.3g; Sugar: 0g; Sodium: 318mg; Fiber: 3.9g

Pinto Beans Balls

Servings:4
Cooking Time: 3 Hours

Ingredients:

- ½ cup pinto beans, cooked
- 1 egg, beaten
- 1 teaspoon garam masala
- 1 onion, diced, roasted
- 2 tablespoons flour
- 1 teaspoon tomato paste
- 1 tablespoon coconut oil

Directions:

1. Mash the pinto beans with the help of the potato masher.
2. Then mix them with egg, garam masala, roasted onion, flour, and tomato paste.
3. Make the small balls from the mixture and put them in the Crock Pot.
4. Add coconut oil.
5. Cook the pinto beans balls for 3 hours on Low.

Nutrition Info:

- InfoPer Serving: 155 calories, 7.3g protein, 21g carbohydrates, 4.9g fat, 4.5g fiber, 41mg cholesterol, 22mg sodium, 409mg potassium.

Creamy White Mushrooms

Servings:4
Cooking Time: 8 Hours

Ingredients:
- 1-pound white mushrooms, chopped
- 1 cup cream
- 1 teaspoon chili flakes
- 1 teaspoon ground black pepper
- 1 tablespoon dried parsley

Directions:
1. Put all ingredients in the Crock Pot.
2. Cook the mushrooms on low for 8 hours.
3. When the mushrooms are cooked, transfer them in the serving bowls and cool for 10-15 minutes.

Nutrition Info:
- InfoPer Serving: 65 calories, 4.1g protein, 6g carbohydrates, 3.7g fat, 1.3g fiber, 11mg cholesterol, 27mg sodium, 396mg potassium.

Vegan Kofte

Servings:4
Cooking Time: 4 Hours

Ingredients:
- 2 eggplants, peeled, boiled
- 1 teaspoon minced garlic
- 1 teaspoon ground cumin
- ¼ teaspoon minced ginger
- ½ cup chickpeas, canned
- 3 tablespoons breadcrumbs
- 1/3 cup water
- 1 tablespoon coconut oil

Directions:
1. Blend the eggplants until smooth.
2. Add minced garlic, ground cumin, minced ginger, chickpeas, and blend the mixture until smooth.
3. Transfer it in the mixing bowl. Add breadcrumbs.
4. Make the small koftes and put them in the Crock Pot.
5. Add coconut oil and close the lid.
6. Cook the meal on Low for 4 hours.

Nutrition Info:
- InfoPer Serving: 212 calories, 8.3g protein, 35.5g carbohydrates, 5.8g fat, 14.3g fiber, 0mg cholesterol, 50mg sodium, 870mg potassium.

Teriyaki Kale

Servings:6
Cooking Time: 30 Minutes

Ingredients:
- 5 cups kale, roughly chopped
- 1/2 cup teriyaki sauce
- 1 teaspoon sesame seeds
- 1 cup of water
- 1 teaspoon garlic powder
- 2 tablespoons coconut oil

Directions:
1. Melt the coconut oil and mix it with garlic powder, water, sesame seeds, and teriyaki sauce.
2. Pour the liquid in the Crock Pot.
3. Add kale and close the lid.
4. Cook the kale on High for 30 minutes.
5. Serve the kale with a small amount of teriyaki liquid.

Nutrition Info:
- InfoPer Serving: 92 calories, 3.3g protein, 10g carbohydrates, 4.8g fat, 1g fiber, 0mg cholesterol, 945mg sodium, 336mg potassium.

Lunch & Dinner Recipes

Lunch & Dinner Recipes

Chipotle Lentil Chili

Servings: 8
Cooking Time: 6 1/2 Hours

Ingredients:
- 2 tablespoons olive oil
- 2 shallots, chopped
- 4 garlic cloves, chopped
- 2 carrots, diced
- 1 chipotle pepper, seeded and chopped
- 1 can (15 oz.) black beans, drained
- 2/3 cup brown lentils
- 1 cup diced tomatoes
- 2 cups vegetable stock
- 1/4 teaspoon chili powder
- 1/4 teaspoon cumin powder
- Salt and pepper to taste
- 1 bay leaf

Directions:
1. Heat the oil in a skillet and add the shallots and garlic. Cook for 2 minutes until softened then transfer the mixture in your Crock Pot.
2. Add the remaining ingredients and season with salt and pepper.
3. Cook on low settings for 6 hours.
4. Serve the chili warm.

Pork Taco Filling

Servings: 8
Cooking Time: 6 1/2 Hours

Ingredients:
- 2 pounds ground pork
- 2 tablespoons canola oil
- 2 shallots, chopped
- 4 garlic cloves, chopped
- 2 chipotle peppers, chopped
- 1 cup ginger beer
- 1 cup pineapple juice
- 1/2 cup chopped cilantro
- 1 pound tomatillos, chopped
- 1 cup frozen corn
- Salt and pepper to taste
- 1 lime, juiced
- Flour tortillas or taco shells for serving

Directions:
1. Heat the oil in a frying pan and add the pork. Cook for a few minutes then transfer in your Crock Pot.
2. Add the shallots, garlic, ginger beer, chipotle peppers, pineapple juice, cilantro, tomatillos, corn and lime juice, as well as salt and pepper.
3. Cover with its lid and cook on low settings for 6 hours.
4. Serve the dish warm, wrapped in flour tortillas or taco shells.

Vegetarian Jambalaya

Servings: 6
Cooking Time: 6 1/2 Hours

Ingredients:

- 1 tablespoon olive oil
- 2 shallots, chopped
- 2 garlic cloves, chopped
- 8 oz. seaman, cubed
- 1 red bell pepper, cored and diced
- 1 celery stalk, sliced
- 2 cups vegetable stock
- 1 teaspoon miso paste
- 1 teaspoon Cajun seasoning
- 1 cup white rice
- 1/2 teaspoon turmeric powder
- Salt and pepper to taste

Directions:

1. Heat the oil in a skillet and add the shallots and garlic. Sauté for 2 minutes until softened then transfer in your Crock Pot.
2. Add the remaining ingredients and season with salt and pepper as needed. Cook on low settings for 6 hours and serve the dish warm and fresh.

Golden Maple Glazed Pork Chops

Servings: 6
Cooking Time: 4 1/4 Hours

Ingredients:

- 6 pork chops
- 2 tablespoons canola oil
- 4 shallots, sliced
- 4 garlic cloves, chopped
- 3 tablespoons maple syrup
- 1/4 cup white wine
- 1/2 teaspoon chili powder
- Salt and pepper to taste

Directions:

1. Heat the oil in a large frying pan and add the pork chops. Fry on high flame for a few minutes on both sides until golden then transfer in your Crock Pot.
2. Add the remaining ingredients and adjust the taste with salt and pepper.
3. Cover with its lid and cook on low settings for 4

hours.
4. The chops are best served warm.

French Veggie Stew

Servings: 6
Cooking Time: 9 Hours

Ingredients:

- 2 yellow onions, chopped
- 1 eggplant, sliced
- 4 zucchinis, sliced
- 2 garlic cloves, minced
- 2 green bell peppers, cut into medium strips
- 6 ounces canned tomato paste
- 2 tomatoes, cut into medium wedges
- 1 teaspoon oregano, dried
- 1 teaspoon sugar
- 1 teaspoon basil, dried
- Salt and black pepper to the taste
- 2 tablespoons parsley, chopped
- ¼ cup olive oil
- A pinch of red pepper flakes, crushed

Directions:

1. In your Crock Pot, mix oil with onions, eggplant, zucchinis, garlic, bell peppers, tomato paste, basil, sugar, oregano, salt and pepper, cover and cook on Low for 9 hours.
2. Add pepper flakes and parsley, stir gently, divide into bowls and serve for lunch.

Nutrition Info:

- Info calories 269, fat 7, fiber 6, carbs 17, protein 4

Thyme Flavored White Bean Pork Cassoulet

Servings: 4
Cooking Time: 4 1/4 Hours

Ingredients:
- 1 pound pork tenderloin, cubed
- 2 tablespoons canola oil
- 1 can (15 oz.) white beans, drained
- 1 celery stalk, sliced
- 1 shallot, chopped
- 1 garlic clove, chopped
- 1 cup diced tomatoes
- 2 thyme sprigs
- 1 cup chicken stock
- Salt and pepper to taste

Directions:
1. Heat the oil in a skillet and add the pork. Cook for a few minutes on all sides until golden brown then transfer in your Crock Pot.
2. Add the rest of the ingredients in a Crock Pot and add salt and pepper to taste.
3. Cook the cassoulet on low settings for 4 hours and serve it warm or chilled.

Salmon And Cilantro Sauce

Servings: 4
Cooking Time: 2 Hours And 30 Minutes

Ingredients:
- 2 garlic cloves, minced
- 4 salmon fillets, boneless
- ¾ cup cilantro, chopped
- 3 tablespoons lime juice
- 1 tablespoon olive oil
- Salt and black pepper to the taste

Directions:
1. Grease your Crock Pot with the oil, add salmon fillets inside skin side down, also add garlic, cilantro, lime juice, salt and pepper, cover and cook on Low for 2 hours and 30 minutes.
2. Divide salmon fillets on plates, drizzle the cilantro sauce all over and serve for lunch.

Nutrition Info:
- Info calories 200, fat 3, fiber 2, carbs 14, protein 8

Cuban Beans

Servings: 6
Cooking Time: 8 1/4 Hours

Ingredients:
- 1 cup dried black beans, rinsed
- 2 cups vegetable stock
- 2 cups water
- 1 cup chopped onion
- 2 red bell peppers, cored and diced
- 1 green bell pepper, cored and diced
- 1 teaspoon fennel seeds
- 1/2 teaspoon cumin seeds
- 1/2 teaspoon ground coriander
- 1 teaspoon sherry wine vinegar
- 1 can fire roasted tomatoes
- 1 green chile, chopped
- Salt and pepper to taste

Directions:
1. Combine the beans and the remaining ingredients in your Crock Pot.
2. Add salt and pepper as needed and cook on low settings for 8 hours.
3. Serve the beans warm in tortillas or over cooked rice.

Lemon Garlic Roasted Chicken

Servings: 6
Cooking Time: 6 1/4 Hours

Ingredients:
- 6 chicken thighs
- 1 lemon, sliced
- 6 garlic cloves, chopped
- 2 tablespoons butter
- 1/2 cup chicken stock
- 1 thyme sprig
- 1 rosemary sprig

Directions:
1. Place the chicken in your crock pot and season it with salt and pepper.
2. Top the chicken with lemon slices, garlic, butter, stock, thyme sprig and rosemary sprig.
3. Cook on low settings for 6 hours.
4. Serve the chicken warm and fresh.

Creamy Brisket

Servings: 2
Cooking Time: 8 Hours

Ingredients:

- 1 tablespoon olive oil
- 1 shallot, chopped
- 2 garlic cloves, mined
- 1 pound beef brisket
- Salt and black pepper to the taste
- ¼ cup beef stock
- 3 tablespoons heavy cream
- 1 tablespoon parsley, chopped

Directions:

1. In your Crock Pot, mix the brisket with the oil and the other ingredients, toss, put the lid on and cook on Low for 8 hours.
2. Transfer the beef to a cutting board, slice, divide between plates and serve with the sauce drizzled all over.

Nutrition Info:

- Info calories 400, fat 10, fiber 4, carbs 15, protein 20

Vegetarian Hungarian Goulash

Servings: 8
Cooking Time: 8 1/2 Hours

Ingredients:

- 2 tablespoons olive oil
- 2 large onions, finely chopped
- 4 garlic cloves, chopped
- 2 carrots, diced
- 1 celery stalk, diced
- 1 can (15 oz.) white beans, drained
- 4 roasted red bell peppers, chopped
- 1 can fire roasted tomatoes
- 1 teaspoon smoked paprika
- 2 tablespoons tomato paste
- 2 pounds potatoes, peeled and cubed
- 2 bay leaves
- 2 cups vegetable stock
- Salt and pepper to taste

Directions:

1. Heat the oil in a skillet and add the onions. Cook for 5 minutes until softened then transfer in your crock pot,
2. Add the remaining ingredients and adjust the taste with salt and pepper.
3. Cook on low settings for 8 hours.
4. Serve the stew warm and fresh.

Bacon Wrapped Beef Tenderloin

Servings: 6
Cooking Time: 8 1/4 Hours

Ingredients:

- 2 pounds beef tenderloin
- 1 teaspoon cumin powder
- 1 teaspoon smoked paprika
- 1 teaspoon dried thyme
- 2 tablespoons olive oil
- 8 slices bacon
- 1 cup beef stock
- Salt and pepper to taste

Directions:

1. Season the beef tenderloin with salt, pepper, cumin powder, paprika and thyme. Drizzle with olive oil and rub the meat well.
2. Wrap the beef in bacon slices and place in your crock pot.
3. Add the stock and cover the pot with its lid.
4. Cook on low settings for 8 hours.
5. When done, slice and serve the tenderloin warm with your favorite side dish.

Beef Strips

Servings: 4
Cooking Time: 6 Hours

Ingredients:
- ½ pound baby mushrooms, sliced
- 1 yellow onion, chopped
- 1 pound beef sirloin steak, cubed
- Salt and black pepper to the taste
- 1/3 cup red wine
- 2 teaspoons olive oil
- 2 cups beef stock
- 1 tablespoon Worcestershire sauce

Directions:
1. In your Crock Pot, mix beef strips with onion, mushrooms, salt, pepper, wine, olive oil, beef stock and Worcestershire sauce, toss, cover and cook on Low for 6 hours.
2. Divide between plates and serve for lunch.

Nutrition Info:
- Info calories 212, fat 7, fiber 1, carbs 8, protein 26

Curried Roasted Pork

Servings: 6
Cooking Time: 6 1/4 Hours

Ingredients:
- 2 pounds pork roast
- 1 1/2 teaspoons curry powder
- 1/2 teaspoon chili powder
- 4 garlic cloves, minced
- 1 teaspoon dried mint
- 1 teaspoon dried basil
- Salt and pepper to taste
- 1 cup coconut milk

Directions:
1. Season the pork roast with salt, pepper, curry powder, chili powder, garlic, mint, basil, salt and pepper to taste.
2. Place the meat in your crock pot and add the coconut milk.
3. Cover and cook on low settings for 6 hours.
4. Serve the pork warm and fresh.

White Bean Chili Over Creamy Grits

Servings: 8
Cooking Time: 6 3/4 Hours

Ingredients:
- 2 cups dried white beans, rinsed
- 2 cups vegetable stock
- 2 cups water
- 1 onion, chopped
- 2 garlic cloves, chopped
- 1 carrot, diced
- 1 celery stalk, diced
- 1 red chili, chopped
- 1/2 teaspoon cumin powder
- 1 cup fire roasted tomatoes
- 1 bay leaf
- 2 cups spinach, shredded
- Salt and pepper to taste
- 1 cup grits
- 2 cups whole milk
- 1 cup grated Cheddar

Directions:
1. Combine the beans, stock, water, onion, garlic, carrot, celery, red chili, tomatoes, cumin powder and bay leaf in your Crock Pot. Top with shredded spinach.
2. Add salt and pepper to taste and cook on low settings for 6 1/2 hours.
3. To make the creamy grits, pour the milk in a saucepan. Bring to a boil and add the grits. Cook on low heat until creamy then remove from heat and add the cheese.
4. Spoon the grits into the serving bowls and top with white bean stew.

Szechuan Roasted Pork

Servings: 8
Cooking Time: 8 1/4 Hours

Ingredients:

- 4 pounds pork shoulder, trimmed
- 1 can (8 oz.) bamboo shoots
- 1 cup water chestnuts, chopped
- 2 shallots, sliced
- 1 tablespoon Worcestershire sauce
- 1/4 cup soy sauce
- 1 tablespoon rice vinegar
- 2 tablespoons red bean paste
- 1 teaspoon sesame oil
- 1 teaspoon garlic powder
- 1 teaspoon hot sauce
- 1 cup chicken stock

Directions:

1. Combine the pork shoulder and the rest of the ingredients in your crock pot.
2. Cover with a lid and cook on low settings for 8 hours.
3. Serve the pork shoulder and the sauce preferably warm and fresh.

Crouton Beef Stew

Servings: 6
Cooking Time: 5 1/4 Hours

Ingredients:

- 1 pound ground beef
- 2 tablespoons canola oil
- 1 shallot, chopped
- 2 garlic cloves, chopped
- 1 can fire roasted tomatoes
- 1 poblano pepper, chopped
- 1 cup beef stock
- 1 cup finely chopped mushrooms
- 2 celery stalks, chopped
- 2 carrots, sliced
- Salt and pepper to taste
- 8 oz. bread croutons

Directions:

1. Heat the oil in a skillet and add the beef. Cook for a few minutes then transfer the meat in your Crock Pot.
2. Add the shallot, garlic, tomatoes, poblano pepper, stock, mushrooms, celery and carrots, as well as salt and pepper. Add salt and pepper as well.
3. Top with bread croutons and cover with a lid.
4. Cook on low settings for 5 hours.
5. Serve the stew warm and fresh.

Soups & Stews Recipes

Soups & Stews Recipes

Lobster Soup

Servings:4
Cooking Time: 2 Hours

Ingredients:
- 4 cups of water
- 1-pound lobster tail, chopped
- ½ cup fresh cilantro, chopped
- 1 cup coconut cream
- 1 teaspoon ground coriander
- 1 garlic clove, diced

Directions:
1. Pour water and coconut cream in the Crock Pot.
2. Add a lobster tail, cilantro, and ground coriander.
3. Then add the garlic clove and close the lid.
4. Cook the lobster soup on High for 2 hours.

Nutrition Info:
- InfoPer Serving: 241 calories, 23g protein, 3.6g carbohydrates, 15.2g fat, 1.4g fiber, 165mg cholesterol, 568mg sodium, 435mg potassium.

Sweet Corn Chowder

Servings: 8
Cooking Time: 6 1/4 Hours

Ingredients:
- 2 shallots, chopped
- 4 medium size potatoes, peeled and cubed1
- 1 celery stalk, sliced
- 1 can (15 oz.) sweet corn, drained
- 2 cups chicken stock
- 2 cups water
- Salt and pepper to taste

Directions:
1. Combine the shallot, potatoes, celery, corn, stock and water in a Crock Pot.
2. Add salt and pepper to taste and cook on low settings for 6 hours.
3. When done, remove a few tablespoons of corn

from the pot then puree the remaining soup in the pot.
4. Pour the soup into serving bowls and top with the reserved corn.
5. Serve warm.

Tuscan Kale And White Bean Soup

Servings: 8
Cooking Time: 8 1/2 Hours

Ingredients:
- 1 1/2 cups dried white beans, rinsed
- 1 sweet onion, chopped
- 2 carrots, diced
- 1 celery stalk, sliced
- 1 teaspoon dried oregano
- 2 cups chicken stock
- 6 cups water
- 1 bay leaf
- 1 teaspoon dried basil
- 1 bunch kale, shredded
- Salt and pepper to taste
- 1 lemon, juiced

Directions:
1. Combine the beans, onion, carrots, celery, dried herbs, stock and water in your Crock Pot.
2. Add salt and pepper to taste and throw in the bay leaf as well.
3. Cook on low settings for 4 hours then add the kale and lemon juice and cook for 4 additional hours.
4. Serve the soup warm or chilled.

Hungarian Borscht

Servings: 8
Cooking Time: 8 1/4 Hours

Ingredients:
- 1 pound beef roast, cubed
- 2 tablespoons canola oil
- 4 medium size beets, peeled and cubed
- 1 can diced tomatoes
- 2 potatoes, peeled and cubed
- 1 sweet onion, chopped
- 2 tablespoons tomato paste
- Salt and pepper to taste
- 4 cups water
- 1 cup vegetable stock
- 1/2 teaspoon cumin seeds
- 1 teaspoon red wine vinegar
- 1 teaspoon honey
- 1/2 teaspoon dried dill
- 1 teaspoon dried parsley

Directions:
1. Heat the oil in a skillet and stir in the beef. Cook for a few minutes on all sides until golden.
2. Transfer the meat in your Crock Pot and add the beets, tomatoes, potatoes, onion and tomato paste.
3. Add salt and pepper, as well as the remaining ingredients and cook on low settings for 8 hours.
4. Serve the soup warm or chilled.

Chunky Pumpkin And Kale Soup

Servings: 6
Cooking Time: 6 1/2 Hours

Ingredients:
- 1 sweet onion, chopped
- 1 red bell pepper, cored and diced
- 1/2 red chili, chopped
- 2 tablespoons olive oil
- 2 cups pumpkin cubes
- 2 cups vegetable stock
- 2 cups water
- 1 bunch kale, shredded
- 1/2 teaspoon cumin seeds
- Salt and pepper to taste

Directions:

1. Combine the onion, bell pepper, chili and olive oil in your Crock Pot.
2. Add the remaining ingredients and adjust the taste with salt and pepper.
3. Mix gently just to evenly distribute the ingredients then cook on low settings for 6 hours.
4. Serve the soup warm or chilled.

Vegetable Chicken Soup

Servings: 8
Cooking Time: 7 1/2 Hours

Ingredients:
- 2 chicken breasts, cubed
- 1 sweet onion, chopped
- 1 garlic clove, chopped
- 2 carrots, diced
- 1 parsnip, diced
- 1 celery stalk, diced
- 1 red bell pepper, cored and diced
- 1 cup diced tomatoes
- Salt and pepper to taste
- 1 cup chicken stock
- 4 cups water
- 1 can condensed cream of chicken soup
- 1 lemon, juiced
- 1 tablespoon chopped parsley

Directions:
1. Combine the chicken and the remaining ingredients in your Crock Pot.
2. Add salt and pepper as needed and cook on low settings for 7 hours.
3. The soup is best served warm, but it can also be re-heated.

Split Pea Sausage Soup

Servings: 8
Cooking Time: 6 1/4 Hours

Ingredients:

- 2 cups split peas, rinsed
- 8 cups water
- 4 Italian sausages, sliced
- 1 sweet onion, chopped
- 2 carrots, diced
- 1 celery stalk, diced
- 1 garlic clove, chopped
- 1 red chili, chopped
- 1/2 teaspoon dried oregano
- 2 tablespoons tomato paste
- Salt and pepper to taste
- 1 lemon, juiced
- 2 tablespoons chopped parsley

Directions:

1. Combine the split peas, water, sausages, onion, carrots, celery, garlic, red chili, oregano and tomato paste in your Crock Pot.
2. Add salt and pepper to taste and cook on low settings for 6 hours.
3. When done, stir in the lemon juice and parsley and serve the soup warm.

Mussel Stew

Servings:4
Cooking Time: 55 Minutes

Ingredients:

- 1-pound mussels
- 2 garlic cloves, diced
- 1 teaspoon smoked paprika
- ½ teaspoon chili powder
- 1 eggplant, chopped
- 1 cup coconut cream
- 1 tablespoon sesame seeds
- 1 teaspoon tomato paste

Directions:

1. Put all ingredients from the list above in the Crock Pot and gently stir.
2. Close the lid and cook the mussel stew for 55 minutes on High.

Nutrition Info:

- InfoPer Serving: 283 calories, 16.7g protein, 16g carbohydrates, 18.3g fat, 6g fiber, 32mg cholesterol, 341mg sodium, 832mg potassium.

Chunky Potato Ham Soup

Servings: 8
Cooking Time: 8 1/2 Hours

Ingredients:

- 2 cups diced ham
- 1 sweet onion, chopped
- 1 garlic clove, chopped
- 1 leek, sliced
- 1 celery stalk, sliced
- 2 carrots, sliced
- 2 pounds potatoes, peeled and cubed
- 1/2 teaspoon dried oregano
- 1/2 teaspoon dried basil
- 2 cups chicken stock
- 3 cups water
- Salt and pepper to taste

Directions:

1. Combine all the ingredients in your Crock Pot.
2. Add salt and pepper to taste and cook on low settings for 8 hours.
3. Serve the soup warm or chilled.

Tomato Fish Soup

Servings: 6
Cooking Time: 3 1/2 Hours

Ingredients:

- 1 shallot, chopped
- 2 garlic cloves, chopped
- 1 tablespoon olive oil
- 4 ripe tomatoes, pureed
- 2 cups vegetable stock
- 1 cup water
- 1 bay leaf
- 1 lemon, juiced
- Salt and pepper to taste
- 1 pound salmon fillets, cubed
- 2 haddock fillets, cubed

Directions:

1. Heat the oil in a skillet and stir in the shallot and garlic. Sauté for 2 minutes until softened then transfer in your Crock Pot.
2. Stir in the tomato puree, stock, water, bay leaf and lemon juice and season with salt and pepper.
3. Cook on high settings for 1 hour then add the fish and continue cooking for 2 additional hours.
4. Serve the soup warm or chilled.

Ham White Bean Soup

Servings: 6
Cooking Time: 2 1/4 Hours

Ingredients:

- 1 tablespoon olive oil
- 4 oz. ham, diced
- 1 sweet onion, chopped
- 2 garlic cloves, chopped
- 1 yellow bell pepper, cored and diced
- 1 red bell pepper, cored and diced
- 1 carrot, diced
- 1 cup diced tomatoes
- 1 can (15 oz.) white beans, drained
- 2 cups chicken stock
- 3 cups water
- Salt and pepper to taste

Directions:

1. Heat the oil in a skillet and add the ham. Cook for

2 minutes then stir in the onion and garlic. Sauté for 2 additional minutes.
2. Transfer the mixture in your Crock Pot and stir in the remaining ingredients.
3. Adjust the taste with salt and pepper and cook on high settings for 2 hours.
4. Serve the soup warm or chilled.

Curried Corn Chowder

Servings: 8
Cooking Time: 8 1/4 Hours

Ingredients:

- 1 sweet onion, chopped
- 2 garlic cloves, chopped
- 2 cups chicken stock
- 1 can (15 oz.) sweet corn, drained
- 2 large potatoes, peeled and cubed
- 1/2 chili pepper, chopped
- 1 1/2 cups whole milk
- Salt and pepper to taste
- 1/4 teaspoon cumin seeds

Directions:

1. Combine the onion, garlic, stock, sweet corn, potatoes and chili pepper in your Crock Pot.
2. Add the remaining ingredients and season with salt and pepper.
3. Cook on low settings for 8 hours.
4. Serve the soup warm and fresh.

Garam Masala Chicken Soup

Servings: 8
Cooking Time: 8 1/4 Hours

Ingredients:
- 8 chicken drumsticks
- 2 tablespoons canola oil
- 1 sweet onion, chopped
- 2 garlic cloves, chopped
- 1 teaspoon garam masala
- 1 pound potatoes, peeled and cubed
- 1 cup coconut milk
- 2 cups chicken stock
- 2 cups water
- 1 cup tomato sauce
- 1 bay leaf
- 1/2 lemongrass stalk, crushed
- 1/2 teaspoon cumin seeds
- Salt and pepper to taste

Directions:
1. Heat the canola oil in a skillet and add the chicken drumsticks. Cook on all sides until golden brown and crusty then transfer in your Crock Pot.
2. Add the remaining ingredients then season with salt and pepper.
3. Cook on low settings for 8 hours.
4. Serve the soup warm or chilled.

Hamburger Soup

Servings: 8
Cooking Time: 7 Hours 15 Minutes

Ingredients:
- 1 pound ground meat, cooked
- 1 can diced tomatoes
- 1 can lima beans
- Salt, to taste
- 2 tablespoons olive oil
- 1 can kidney beans
- 1 can mixed vegetables
- 1½ teaspoons red chili powder
- 1 can beef broth

Directions:
1. Put olive oil and ground meat in a crock pot and cook for about 5 minutes.

2. Transfer the remaining ingredients into the crock pot and cover the lid.
3. Cook on LOW for about 7 hours and ladle out into serving bowl to serve hot.

Nutrition Info:
- Info Calories: 262 Fat: 14.4g Carbohydrates: 12.2g

Hearty Turkey Chili

Servings: 5
Cooking Time: 8 Hours 15 Minutes

Ingredients:
- ¼ cup olive oil
- 1 pound ground turkey breast
- ½ teaspoon salt
- 1 can white beans, drained and rinsed
- 2 teaspoons dried marjoram
- 1 large onion, chopped
- 1 green pepper, chopped
- 1 can diced tomatoes
- 2 tablespoons chili powder
- 4 garlic cloves, minced
- 1 can no-salt-added tomatoes

Directions:
1. Put olive oil, green peppers, onions and garlic in the crock pot and sauté for about 3 minutes.
2. Add rest of the ingredients and cover the lid.
3. Cook on LOW for about 8 hours and dish out in a bowl to serve hot.

Nutrition Info:
- Info Calories: 350 Fat: 17.6g Carbohydrates: 18.1g

Tomato Beef Soup

Servings: 8
Cooking Time: 8 1/4 Hours

Ingredients:

- 2 tablespoons olive oil
- 2 bacon slices, chopped
- 2 pounds beef roast, cubed
- 2 sweet onions, chopped
- 2 tomatoes, peeled and diced
- 2 cups tomato sauce
- 1 cup beef stock
- 3 cups water
- Salt and pepper to taste
- 1 thyme sprig
- 1 rosemary sprig

Directions:

1. Heat the oil in a skillet and add the bacon. Cook until crisp and stir in the beef roast. Cook for 5 minutes on all sides.
2. Transfer the beet and bacon in a Crock Pot.
3. Add the remaining ingredients and adjust the taste with salt and pepper.
4. Cook on low settings for 8 hours.
5. Serve the soup warm or chilled.

Garlicky Spinach Soup With Herbed Croutons

Servings: 6
Cooking Time: 2 1/4 Hours

Ingredients:

- 1 pound fresh spinach, shredded
- 1/2 teaspoon dried oregano
- 1 shallot, chopped
- 4 garlic cloves, chopped
- 1/2 celery stalk, sliced
- 2 cups water
- 2 cups chicken stock
- Salt and pepper to taste
- 1 lemon, juiced
- 1/2 cup half and half
- 10 oz. one-day old bread, cubed
- 3 tablespoons olive oil
- 1 teaspoon dried basil
- 1 teaspoon dried marjoram

Directions:

1. Combine the spinach, oregano, shallot, garlic and celery in your Crock Pot.
2. Add the water, stock and lemon juice, as well as salt and pepper to taste and cook on high settings for 2 hours.
3. While the soup is cooking, place the bread cubes in a large baking tray and drizzle with olive oil. Sprinkle with salt and pepper and cook in the preheated oven at 375F for 10-12 minutes until crispy and golden.
4. When the soup is done, puree it with an immersion blender, adding the half and half while doing so.
5. Serve the soup warm, topped with herbed croutons.

Poultry Recipes

Poultry Recipes

Chicken And Mustard Sauce

Servings: 3
Cooking Time: 4 Hours

Ingredients:
- 8 bacon strips, cooked and chopped
- 1/3 cup Dijon mustard
- Salt and black pepper to the taste
- 1 cup yellow onion, chopped
- 1 tablespoon olive oil
- 1 and ½ cups chicken stock
- 3 chicken breasts, skinless and boneless
- ¼ teaspoon sweet paprika

Directions:
1. In a bowl, mix paprika with mustard, salt and pepper and stir well.
2. Spread this on chicken breasts and massage.
3. Heat up a pan with the oil over medium-high heat, add chicken breasts, cook for 2 minutes on each side and transfer to your Crock Pot.
4. Add stock, bacon and onion, stir, cover and cook on High for 4 hours.
5. Divide chicken between plates, drizzle mustard sauce all over and serve.

Nutrition Info:
- Info calories 223, fat 8, fiber 1, carbs 13, protein 26

Chicken Stuffed With Beans

Servings: 12
Cooking Time: 10 Hours

Ingredients:
- 21 oz. whole chicken
- 1 chili pepper, chopped
- 1 cup soybeans, canned
- 2 red onion, peeled and diced
- 1 carrot, peeled and diced
- 1 tsp onion powder
- 1 tsp cilantro, chopped
- 1 tsp oregano
- 1 tsp apple cider vinegar
- 1 tsp olive oil
- 1 tbsp dried basil
- 1 tsp paprika
- ¼ tsp ground red pepper
- ½ cup fresh dill
- 2 potatoes, peeled and diced
- 4 tbsp tomato sauce

Directions:
1. Blend chili pepper, onion powder, cilantro, oregano, olive oil, red pepper, tomato sauce, dill, paprika, basil, and vinegar in a blender.
2. Stuff the whole chicken with soybeans, and vegetables.
3. Brush it with the blender spice-chili mixture liberally.
4. Place the spiced chicken in the Crock Pot and pour the remaining spice mixture over it.
5. Put the cooker's lid on and set the cooking time to 10 hours on Low settings.
6. Slice and serve.

Nutrition Info:
- Info Per Serving: Calories: 186, Total Fat: 4.1g, Fiber: 5g, Total Carbs: 27.23g, Protein: 11g

Chicken Enchilada

Servings: 10
Cooking Time: 8 Hours

Ingredients:
- 4 ½ cups shredded chicken
- 1 ¼ cup sour cream
- 1 can sugar-free green enchilada sauce
- 4 cups Monterey jack cheese
- ½ cup cilantro, chopped

Directions:
1. Place the shredded chicken in the crockpot.
2. Add in the sour cream and enchilada sauce.
3. Sprinkle with Monterey jack cheese.
4. Close the lid and cook on low for 8 hours or on high for 6 hours.
5. An hour before the cooking time ends, sprinkle with cilantro.

Nutrition Info:
- Info   Calories per serving: 469; Carbohydrates: 5g; Protein: 34g; Fat:29 g; Sugar:2.2 g; Sodium: 977mg; Fiber: 1g

Tender Duck Fillets

Servings: 3
Cooking Time: 8 Hours

Ingredients:
- 1 tablespoon butter
- 1 teaspoon dried rosemary
- 1 teaspoon ground nutmeg
- 9 oz duck fillet
- 1 cup of water

Directions:
1. Slice the fillet.
2. Then melt the butter in the skillet.
3. Add sliced duck fillet and roast it for 2-3 minutes per side on medium heat.
4. Transfer the roasted duck fillet and butter in the Crock Pot.
5. Add dried rosemary, ground nutmeg, and water.
6. Close the lid and cook the meal on Low for 8 hours.

Nutrition Info:
- InfoPer Serving: 145 calories, 25.2g protein, 0.6g carbohydrates, 4.7g fat, 0.3g fiber, 10mg cholesterol, 158mg sodium, 61mg potassium.

Turkey And Scallions Mix

Servings: 2
Cooking Time: 7 Hours

Ingredients:
- 1 pound turkey breasts, skinless, boneless and cubed
- 1 tablespoon avocado oil
- ½ cup tomato sauce
- ½ cup chicken stock
- ½ teaspoon sweet paprika
- 4 scallions, chopped
- 1 tablespoons lemon zest, grated
- 1 tablespoon lemon juice
- A pinch of salt and black pepper
- 1 tablespoon chives, chopped

Directions:
1. In your Crock Pot, mix the turkey with the oil, tomato sauce and the other ingredients, toss, put the lid on and cook on Low for 7 hours.
2. Divide everything between plates and serve.

Nutrition Info:
- Info calories 234, fat 12, fiber 3, carbs 5, protein 7

Simple Buttered Rosemary Chicken Breasts

Servings:4
Cooking Time: 6 Hours

Ingredients:
- 5 tablespoons butter
- 4 boneless chicken breasts
- Salt and pepper to taste
- 1 tablespoon parsley
- 1 teaspoon rosemary

Directions:
1. Melt the butter in the skillet.
2. Season chicken with salt and pepper to taste. Brown all sides of the chicken for 3 minutes.
3. Transfer into the crockpot and sprinkle with parsley and rosemary.
4. Cook on low for 6 hours or on high for 5 hours.

Nutrition Info:
- Info Calories per serving: 459; Carbohydrates: 1.17g; Protein: 61.6g; Fat: 21.5g; Sugar: 0g; Sodium: 527mg; Fiber: 0.6g

Cashew Thai Chicken

Servings: 6
Cooking Time: 4 Hrs

Ingredients:
- 1 ½ lb. chicken breast, boneless, skinless and cubed
- 1 tbsp olive oil
- 3 tbsp soy sauce
- 2 tbsp flour
- Salt and black pepper to the taste
- 1 tbsp ketchup
- 2 tbsp white vinegar
- 1 tsp ginger, grated
- 2 tbsp sugar
- 2 garlic cloves, minced
- To serve:
- ½ cup cashews, chopped
- 1 green onion, chopped

Directions:
1. Coat the chicken pieces with flour, salt, and black pepper.

2. Take oil in a nonstick skillet and place it over medium-high heat.
3. Sear the chicken for 5 minutes per side in the skillet.
4. Transfer the chicken to the Crock Pot along with ketchup and remaining ingredients.
5. Put the cooker's lid on and set the cooking time to 5 hours on Low settings.
6. Garnish with green onion and cashews.
7. Serve warm.

Nutrition Info:
- Info Per Serving: Calories 200, Total Fat 3g, Fiber 2g, Total Carbs 13g, Protein 12g

Tomato Chicken

Servings: 4
Cooking Time: 9 Hours

Ingredients:
- 1 lb. chicken wings
- 1 cup canned tomatoes, diced
- ½ cup fresh tomatoes
- 1 cup fresh parsley
- 1 tsp salt
- 1 tsp ground cinnamon
- 1 cup onion
- 1 tbsp olive oil
- 1 tbsp red pepper

Directions:
1. Blend tomatoes in a blender then add parsley, salt, red pepper, and onion.
2. Puree this mixture again then pour it into the Crock Pot.
3. Add chicken wings to the cooker.
4. Put the cooker's lid on and set the cooking time to 8 hours on Low settings.
5. Mix well and serve warm.

Nutrition Info:
- Info Per Serving: Calories: 202, Total Fat: 7.7g, Fiber: 2g, Total Carbs: 6.47g, Protein: 26g

Bbq Pulled Chicken

Servings:3
Cooking Time:8 Hours

Ingredients:
- 12 oz chicken breast, skinless, boneless
- ½ cup BBQ sauce
- 1 teaspoon dried rosemary
- 1 cup of water

Directions:
1. Pour water in the Crock Pot.
2. Add chicken breast and dried rosemary. Cook the chicken on High for 5 hours.
3. Then drain the water and shred the chicken with the help of the fork.
4. Add BBQ sauce, carefully mix the chicken and cook it on Low for 3 hours.

Nutrition Info:
- InfoPer Serving: 193 calories, 24.1g protein, 15.4g carbohydrates, 3g fat, 0.4g fiber, 73mg cholesterol, 527mg sodium, 511mg potassium.

Algerian Chicken

Servings:2
Cooking Time: 4 Hours

Ingredients:
- 6 oz chicken breast, skinless, boneless, sliced
- 1 teaspoon peanut oil
- 1 teaspoon harissa
- 1 teaspoon tomato paste
- 1 tablespoon sesame oil
- 1 cup tomatoes, canned
- ¼ cup of water

Directions:
1. Mix tomato paste with harissa, peanut oil, and sesame oil. Whisk the mixture and mix it with sliced chicken breast.
2. After this, transfer the chicken in the Crock Pot in one layer.
3. Add water and close the lid.
4. Cook the chicken on High for 4 hours.

Nutrition Info:
- InfoPer Serving: 204 calories, 19.1 protein, 5g carbohydrates, 11.8g fat, 1.2g fiber, 55mg cholesterol, 81mg sodium, 555mg potassium.

Red Sauce Chicken Soup

Servings: 4
Cooking Time: 3 Hours

Ingredients:
- 3 tbsp butter, melted
- 4 oz. cream cheese
- 2 cups chicken meat, cooked and shredded
- 1/3 cup red sauce
- 4 cups chicken stock
- Salt and black pepper to the taste
- ½ cup sour cream
- ¼ cup celery, chopped

Directions:
1. Blend stock with red sauce, sour cream, black pepper, butter, cream cheese, and salt in a blender.
2. Transfer this red sauce mixture to the Crock Pot along with chicken and celery.
3. Put the cooker's lid on and set the cooking time to 3 hours on High settings.
4. Serve warm.

Nutrition Info:
- Info Per Serving: Calories: 400, Total Fat: 23g, Fiber: 5g, Total Carbs: 15g, Protein: 30g

Chicken Pepper Chili

Servings: 4
Cooking Time: 7 Hrs

Ingredients:
- 16 oz. salsa
- 8 chicken thighs
- 1 yellow onion, chopped
- 16 oz. canned tomatoes, chopped
- 1 red bell pepper, chopped
- 2 tbsp chili powder

Directions:
1. Add salsa and all other ingredients to the Crock Pot.
2. Put the cooker's lid on and set the cooking time to 7 hours on Low settings.
3. Serve warm.

Nutrition Info:
- Info Per Serving: Calories 250, Total Fat 3g, Fiber 3g, Total Carbs 14g, Protein 8g

Chicken Soufflé

Servings:6
Cooking Time: 3.5 Hours

Ingredients:
- 1-pound ground chicken
- 1 teaspoon dried oregano
- 1 teaspoon dried sage
- 1 teaspoon butter, softened
- 1 teaspoon salt
- ½ cup cream
- 4 eggs, beaten
- 2 oz provolone cheese, shredded

Directions:
1. Mix ground chicken with dried oregano, sage, butter, and salt.
2. Then mix the ground mixture with eggs and transfer in the ramekins.
3. Add cream and cheese.
4. Cover the ramekins with foil and transfer in the Crock Pot.
5. Cook the soufflé on High for 3.5 hours.

Nutrition Info:

- InfoPer Serving: 238 calories, 28.2g protein, carbohydrates, 12.8g fat, 0.2g fiber, 188mg cholesterol, 587mg sodium, 249mg potassium.

Red Chicken Soup

Servings: 4
Cooking Time: 3 Hours

Ingredients:
- 3 tablespoons butter, melted
- 4 ounces cream cheese
- 2 cups chicken meat, cooked and shredded
- 1/3 cup red sauce
- 4 cups chicken stock
- Salt and black pepper to the taste
- ½ cup sour cream
- ¼ cup celery, chopped

Directions:
1. In your blender, mix stock with red sauce, cream cheese, butter, salt, pepper and sour cream, pulse well and transfer to your Crock Pot.
2. Add celery and chicken, stir, cover and cook on High for 3 hours.
3. Divide into bowls and serve.

Nutrition Info:
- Info calories 400, fat 23, fiber 5, carbs 15, protein 30

d Chicken Saute

1.3g
ster

Hours

- ot, chopped
- on cobs, roughly chopped
- of water
- ound chicken fillet, chopped
- teaspoon Italian seasonings
- 1 teaspoon salt

Directions:

1. Put all ingredients from the list above in the Crock Pot.

2. Close the lid and cook the meal on Low for 8 hours.

Nutrition Info:

- InfoPer Serving: 308 calories, 35.3g protein, 18.8g carbohydrates, 10.5g fat, 0.7g fiber, 105mg cholesterol, 714mg sodium, 544mg potassium.

Chicken Vegetable Curry

Servings:6

Cooking Time: 8 Hours

Ingredients:

- 1 tablespoon butter
- 1-pound chicken breasts, bones removed
- 1 package frozen vegetable mix
- 1 cup water
- 2 tablespoons curry powder

Directions:

1. Place all ingredients in the crockpot.

2. Stir to combine everything.

3. Close the lid and cook on low for 8 hours or on high for 6 hours.

Nutrition Info:

- Info Calories per serving: 273; Carbohydrates: 6.1g; Protein:21 g; Fat: 10g; Sugar: 0.1g; Sodium: 311mg; Fiber: 4g

Lemongrass Chicken Thighs

Servings:6

Cooking Time: 4 Hours

Ingredients:

- 6 chicken thighs
- 1 tablespoon dried sage
- 1 teaspoon salt
- 1 teaspoon ground paprika
- 2 tablespoons sesame oil
- 1 cup of water

Directions:

1. Mix dried sage with salt, and ground paprika.

2. Then rub the chicken thighs with the sage mixture and transfer in the Crock Pot.

3. Sprinkle the chicken with sesame oil and water.

4. Close the chicken on High for 4 hours.

Nutrition Info:

- InfoPer Serving: 320 calories, 42.3g protein, 0.4g carbohydrates, 15.4g fat, 0.3g fiber, 130mg cholesterol, 514mg sodium, 367mg potassium.

Fish & Seafood Recipes

Fish & Seafood Recipes

Clam Chowder

s: 4

ng Time: 2 Hours

gredients:
- 1 cup celery stalks, chopped
- Salt and black pepper to the taste
- 1 teaspoon thyme, ground
- 2 cups chicken stock
- 14 ounces canned baby clams
- 2 cups whipping cream
- 1 cup onion, chopped
- 13 bacon slices, chopped

Directions:
1. Heat up a pan over medium heat, add bacon slices, brown them and transfer to a bowl.
2. Heat up the same pan over medium heat, add celery and onion, stir and cook for 5 minutes.
3. Transfer everything to your Crock Pot, also add bacon, baby clams, salt, pepper, stock, thyme and whipping cream, stir and cook on High for 2 hours.
4. Divide into bowls and serve.

Nutrition Info:
- Info calories 420, fat 22, fiber 0, carbs 5, protein 25

Trout Cakes

Servings:2
Cooking Time: 2 Hours

Ingredients:
- 7 oz trout fillet, diced
- 1 tablespoon semolina
- 1 teaspoon dried oregano
- ¼ teaspoon ground black pepper
- 1 teaspoon cornflour
- 1 egg, beaten
- 1/3 cup water
- 1 teaspoon sesame oil

Directions:

1. In the bowl mix diced trout, semolina, dried oregano, ground black pepper, and cornflour.
2. Then add egg and carefully mix the mixture.
3. Heat the sesame oil well.
4. Then make the fish cakes and put them in the hot oil.
5. Roast them for 1 minute per side and transfer in the Crock Pot.
6. Add water and cook the trout cakes for 2 hours on High.

Nutrition Info:
- InfoPer Serving: 266 calories, 30g protein, 5.6g carbohydrates, 13.1g fat, 0.7g fiber, 155mg cholesterol, 99mg sodium, 519mg potassium.

Garlic Sardines

Servings:4
Cooking Time: 3 Hours

Ingredients:
- 1-pound sardines, cleaned
- 1 teaspoon garlic powder
- ½ teaspoon ground black pepper
- ¼ cup cornflour
- 1 tablespoon avocado oil
- ¼ cup of water

Directions:
1. Pour water in the Crock Pot.
2. Add avocado oil.
3. Then sprinkle the sardines with garlic powder, ground black pepper, and cornflour.
4. Put the fish in the Crock Pot and close the lid.
5. Cook the sardines on High for 3 hours.

Nutrition Info:
- InfoPer Serving: 280 calories, 27.6g protein, 6.5g carbohydrates, 13.7g fat, 0.8g fiber, 161mg cholesterol, 574mg sodium, 495mg potassium

Herbed Shrimps

Servings: 4
Cooking Time: 40 Minutes

Ingredients:

- 4 tbsp fresh dill
- ¼ cup pineapple juice
- 2 tbsp sugar
- 3 tbsp mango puree
- 1 tbsp butter
- 1 lb. shrimp, peeled
- 1 tsp ground ginger
- ½ tsp lemon juice
- 1 tbsp tomato juice
- 1 cup of water
- ½ tsp sage

Directions:

1. Add shrimp, water, and sage to the insert of Crock Pot.
2. Put the cooker's lid on and set the cooking time to 20 minutes on High settings.
3. Meanwhile, mix melted butter, mango puree, pineapple juice, sugar, lemon juice, ginger ground, dill and tomatoes juice in a bowl.
4. Add this mixture to the shrimp in the Crock Pot.
5. Put the cooker's lid on and set the cooking time to 20 minutes on High settings.
6. Serve warm.

Nutrition Info:

- Info Per Serving: Calories: 192, Total Fat: 5.4g, Fiber: 2g, Total Carbs: 12.18g, Protein: 24g

Shrimp Chicken Jambalaya

Servings: 8
Cooking Time: 4 Hrs. 30 Minutes

Ingredients:

- 1 lb. chicken breast, chopped
- 1 lb. shrimp, peeled and deveined
- 2 tbsp extra virgin olive oil
- 1 lb. sausage, chopped
- 2 cups onions, chopped
- 1 and ½ cups of rice
- 2 tbsp garlic, chopped
- 2 cups green, yellow and red bell peppers, chopped

- 3 and ½ cups chicken stock
- 1 tbsp Creole seasoning
- 1 tbsp Worcestershire sauce
- 1 cup tomatoes, crushed

Directions:

1. Brush the insert of your Crock Pot with oil.
2. Toss in sausage, chicken, bell peppers, garlic, onion, rice, tomatoes, stock, Worcestershire sauce, and seasoning.
3. Put the cooker's lid on and set the cooking time to 4 hours on High settings.
4. Stir in shrimp and cook for another 30 minutes on High settings.
5. Serve warm.

Nutrition Info:

- Info Per Serving: Calories: 251, Total Fat: 10g, Fiber: 3g, Total Carbs: 20g, Protein: 25g

Braised Lobster

Servings:4
Cooking Time: 3 Hours

Ingredients:

- 2-pound lobster, cleaned
- 1 cup of water
- 1 teaspoon Italian seasonings

Directions:

1. Put all ingredients in the Crock Pot.
2. Close the lid and cook the lobster in High for 3 hours.
3. Remove the lobster from the Crock Pot and cool it till room temperature

Nutrition Info:

- InfoPer Serving: 206 calories, 43.1g protein, 0.1g carbohydrates, 2.2g fat, 0g fiber, 332mg cholesterol, 1104mg sodium, 524mg potassium.

Almond-crusted Tilapia

Servings: 4
Cooking Time: 4 Hours

Ingredients:
- 2 tablespoons olive oil
- 1 cup chopped almonds
- ¼ cup ground flaxseed
- 4 tilapia fillets
- Salt and pepper to taste

Directions:
1. Line the bottom of the crockpot with a foil.
2. Grease the foil with the olive oil.
3. In a mixing bowl, combine the almonds and flaxseed.
4. Season the tilapia with salt and pepper to taste.
5. Dredge the tilapia fillets with the almond and flaxseed mixture.
6. Place neatly in the foil-lined crockpot.
7. Close the lid and cook on high for 2 hours and on low for 4 hours.

Nutrition Info:
- Info Calories per serving: 233; Carbohydrates: 4.6g; Protein: 25.5g; Fat: 13.3g; Sugar: 0.4g; Sodium: 342mg; Fiber: 1.9g

Nutmeg Trout

Servings: 4
Cooking Time: 3 Hours

Ingredients:
- 1 tablespoon ground nutmeg
- 1 tablespoon butter, softened
- 1 teaspoon dried cilantro
- 1 teaspoon dried oregano
- 1 teaspoon fish sauce
- 4 trout fillets
- ½ cup of water

Directions:
1. In the shallow bowl mix butter with cilantro, dried oregano, and fish sauce. Add ground nutmeg and whisk the mixture.
2. Then grease the fish fillets with nutmeg mixture and put in the Crock Pot.
3. Add remaining butter mixture and water.
4. Cook the fish on high for 3 hours.

Nutrition Info:
- InfoPer Serving: 154 calories, 16.8g protein, 1.2g carbohydrates, 8.8g fat, 0.5g fiber, 54mg cholesterol, 178mg sodium, 305mg potassium.

Oregano Shrimp Bowls

Servings: 2
Cooking Time: 1 Hour

Ingredients:
- 1 pound shrimp, peeled and deveined
- ½ cup cherry tomatoes, halved
- ½ cup baby spinach
- 1 tablespoon lime juice
- 1 tablespoon oregano, chopped
- ¼ cup fish stock
- ½ teaspoon sweet paprika
- 2 garlic cloves, chopped
- A pinch of salt and black pepper

Directions:
1. In your Crock Pot, mix the shrimp with the cherry tomatoes, spinach and the other ingredients, toss, put the lid on and cook on High for 1 hour.
2. Divide everything between plates and serve.

Nutrition Info:
- Info calories 211, fat 13, fiber 2, carbs 7, protein 11

Balsamic-glazed Salmon

Servings: 7
Cooking Time: 1.5 Hrs.

Ingredients:
- 5 tbsp brown sugar
- 2 tbsp sesame seeds
- 1 tbsp balsamic vinegar
- 1 tbsp butter
- 3 tbsp water
- 1 tsp salt
- ½ tsp ground black pepper
- 1 tsp ground paprika
- 1 tsp turmeric
- ¼ tsp fresh rosemary
- 1 tsp olive oil
- 21 oz salmon fillet

Directions:
1. Whisk rosemary, black pepper, salt, turmeric, and paprika in a small bowl.
2. Rub the salmon fillet with this spice's mixture.
3. Grease a suitable pan with olive oil and place it over medium-high heat.
4. Place the spiced salmon fillet in the hot pan and sear it for 3 minutes per side.
5. Add butter, sesame seeds, brown sugar, balsamic vinegar, and water to the insert of the Crock Pot.
6. Put the cooker's lid on and set the cooking time to 30 minutes on High settings.
7. Stir this sugar mixture occasionally.
8. Place the salmon fillet in the Crock Pot.
9. Put the cooker's lid on and set the cooking time to 1 hour on Low settings.
10. Serve warm.

Nutrition Info:
- Info Per Serving: Calories: 170, Total Fat: 9.9g, Fiber: 1g, Total Carbs: 1.43g, Protein: 18g

Shrimp With Spinach

Servings: 2
Cooking Time: 1 Hour

Ingredients:
- 1 pound shrimp, peeled and deveined
- 1 cup baby spinach
- ¼ cup tomato passata
- ½ cup chicken stock
- 3 scallions, chopped
- 1 tablespoon olive oil
- ½ teaspoon sweet paprika
- A pinch of salt and black pepper
- 1 tablespoon chives, chopped

Directions:
1. In your Crock Pot, mix the shrimp with the spinach, tomato passata and the other ingredients, toss, put the lid on and cook on High for 1 hour.
2. Divide the mix between plates and serve.

Nutrition Info:
- Info calories 200, fat 13, fiber 3, carbs 6, protein 11

Lobster Colorado

Servings: 4
Cooking Time: 6 Hours 30 Minutes

Ingredients:
- ½ teaspoon garlic powder
- Salt and black pepper, to taste
- 4 (8 ounce) beef tenderloin
- ½ cup butter, divided
- 4 slices bacon
- 8 ounces lobster tail, cleaned and chopped
- 1 teaspoon Old Bay Seasoning

Directions:
1. Season the beef tenderloins with garlic powder, salt and black pepper.
2. Transfer the beef tenderloins in the crock pot and add butter.
3. Cover and cook on LOW for about 3 hours.
4. Add lobster and bacon and cover the lid.
5. Cook on LOW for another 3 hours and dish out to serve hot.

Nutrition Info:
- Info Calories: 825 Fat: 52.2g Carbohydrates: 0.6g

Salmon And Green Onions Mix

Servings: 4
Cooking Time: 2 Hours

Ingredients:
- 1 green onions bunch, halved
- 10 tablespoons lemon juice
- 4 salmon fillets, boneless
- Salt and black pepper to the taste
- 2 tablespoons avocado oil

Directions:
1. Grease your Crock Pot with the oil, add salmon, top with onion, lemon juice, salt and pepper, cover, cook on High for 2 hours, divide everything between plates and serve.

Nutrition Info:
- Info calories 260, fat 3, fiber 1, carbs 14, protein 14

Shrimp, Salmon And Tomatoes Mix

Servings: 2
Cooking Time: 1 Hour And 30 Minutes

Ingredients:
- 1 pound shrimp, peeled and deveined
- ½ pound salmon fillets, boneless and cubed
- 1 cup cherry tomatoes, halved
- ½ cup chicken stock
- ½ teaspoon chili powder
- ½ teaspoon rosemary, dried
- A pinch of salt and black pepper
- 1 tablespoon parsley, chopped
- 2 tablespoons tomato sauce
- 2 garlic cloves, minced

Directions:
1. In your Crock Pot, combine the shrimp with the salmon, tomatoes and the other ingredients, toss gently, put the lid on and cook on High for 1 hour and 30 minutes.
2. Divide the mix into bowls and serve.

Nutrition Info:
- Info calories 232, fat 7, fiber 3, carbs 7, protein 9

Five-spice Tilapia

Servings:4
Cooking Time: 5 Hours

Ingredients:
- 4 tilapia fillets
- 1 teaspoon Chinese five-spice powder
- 1 tablespoon sesame oil
- ¼ cup gluten-free soy sauce
- 3 scallions, thinly sliced

Directions:
1. Season the tilapia fillets with the Chinese five-spice powder.
2. Place sesame oil in the crockpot and arrange the fish on top.
3. Cook on high for 2 hours and on low for 4 hours.
4. Halfway through the cooking time, flip the fish to slightly brown the other side.
5. Once cooking time is done, add the soy sauce and scallion and continue cooking for another hour.

Nutrition Info:
- Info Calories per serving: 153; Carbohydrates: 0.9g; Protein: 25.8g; Fat: 5.6g; Sugar: 0g; Sodium: 424mg; Fiber: 0g

Crab Bake

Servings: 4
Cooking Time: 1.5 Hours

Ingredients:
- 1 cup Cheddar cheese, shredded
- 1-pound crab meat, cooked, chopped
- 1 teaspoon white pepper
- 1 teaspoon dried cilantro
- 1 cup cream

Directions:
1. Put crab meat in the Crock Pot and flatten it in one layer.
2. Sprinkle it with white pepper and dried cilantro.
3. After this, pour the cream and sprinkle the crab meat with Cheddar cheese.
4. Close the lid and cook the meal on High for 1.5 hours.

Nutrition Info:
- InfoPer Serving: 255 calories, 21.8g protein, 4.6g carbohydrates, 14.7g fat, 0.1g fiber, 102mg cholesterol, 904mg sodium, 57mg potassium.

Ginger Tuna

Servings: 2
Cooking Time: 2 Hours

Ingredients:
- 1 pound tuna fillets, boneless and roughly cubed
- 1 tablespoon ginger, grated
- 1 red onion, chopped
- 2 teaspoons olive oil
- Juice of 1 lime
- ¼ cup chicken stock
- 1 tablespoon chives, chopped
- A pinch of salt and black pepper

Directions:
1. In your Crock Pot, mix the tuna with the ginger, onion and the other ingredients, toss, put the lid on and cook on High for 2 hours.
2. Divide the mix into bowls and serve.

Nutrition Info:
- Info calories 200, fat 11, fiber 4, carbs 5, protein 12

Snack Recipes

Snack Recipes

Beer And Cheese Dip

Servings: 10
Cooking Time: 1 Hour

Ingredients:
- 12 ounces cream cheese
- 6 ounces beer
- 4 cups cheddar cheese, shredded
- 1 tablespoon chives, chopped

Directions:
1. In your Crock Pot, mix cream cheese with beer and cheddar, stir, cover and cook on Low for 1 hour.
2. Stir your dip, add chives, divide into bowls and serve.

Nutrition Info:
- Info calories 212, fat 4, fiber 7, carbs 16, protein 5

Peanut Snack

Servings: 4
Cooking Time: 1 Hour And 30 Minutes

Ingredients:
- 1 cup peanuts
- 1 cup chocolate peanut butter
- 12 ounces dark chocolate chips
- 12 ounces white chocolate chips

Directions:
1. In your Crock Pot, mix peanuts with peanut butter, dark and white chocolate chips, cover and cook on Low for 1 hour and 30 minutes.
2. Divide this mix into small muffin cups, leave aside to cool down and serve as a snack.

Nutrition Info:
- Info calories 200, fat 4, fiber 6, carbs 10, protein 5

Cheesy Potato Dip

Servings: 12
Cooking Time: 5 Hours

Ingredients:
- 1 cup heavy cream
- 1 cup milk
- 2 tbsp cornstarch
- 5 medium potatoes, peeled and diced
- 5 oz. Cheddar cheese, chopped
- 1 cup fresh cilantro
- 1 tsp salt
- 1 tsp black pepper
- 1 tsp paprika
- ½ tsp onion powder
- 1 tbsp garlic powder
- ¼ tsp oregano

Directions:
1. Add milk, cream, potatoes, salt, paprika, onion powder, oregano, garlic powder, and black pepper to the Crock Pot.
2. Put the cooker's lid on and set the cooking time to 3 hours on High settings.
3. Stir in cilantro and cheese to the cooked potatoes.
4. Put the cooker's lid on and set the cooking time to 2 hours on High settings.
5. Mix well and serve.

Nutrition Info:
- Info Per Serving: Calories: 196, Total Fat: 5.6g, Fiber: 4g, Total Carbs: 31.58g, Protein: 6g

Bourbon Sausage Bites

Servings: 12
Cooking Time: 3 Hours And 5 Minutes

Ingredients:
- 1/3 cup bourbon
- 1 pound smoked sausage, sliced
- 12 ounces chili sauce
- ¼ cup brown sugar
- 2 tablespoons yellow onion, grated

Directions:
1. Heat up a pan over medium-high heat, add sausage slices, brown them for 2 minutes on each side, drain them on paper towels and transfer to your Crock Pot.
2. Add chili sauce, sugar, onion and bourbon, toss to coat, cover and cook on Low for 3 hours.
3. Divide into bowls and serve as a snack.

Nutrition Info:
- Info calories 190, fat 11, fiber 1, carbs 12, protein 5

Lentils Hummus

Servings: 2
Cooking Time: 4 Hours

Ingredients:
- 1 cup chicken stock
- 1 cup canned lentils, drained
- 2 tablespoons tahini paste
- ¼ teaspoon onion powder
- ¼ cup heavy cream
- A pinch of salt and black pepper
- ¼ teaspoon turmeric powder
- 1 teaspoon lemon juice

Directions:
1. In your Crock Pot, mix the lentils with the stock, onion powder, salt and pepper, toss, put the lid on and cook on High for 4 hours.
2. Drain the lentils, transfer to your blender, add the rest of the ingredients, pulse well, divide into bowls and serve.

Nutrition Info:
- Info calories 192, fat 7, fiber 7, carbs 12, protein 4

Garlic Parmesan Dip

Servings: 7
Cooking Time: 6 Hours

Ingredients:
- 10 oz. garlic cloves, peeled
- 5 oz. Parmesan
- 1 cup cream cheese
- 1 tsp cayenne pepper
- 1 tbsp dried dill
- 1 tsp turmeric
- ½ tsp butter

Directions:
1. Add garlic cloves, cream cheese and all other ingredients to the Crock Pot.
2. Put the cooker's lid on and set the cooking time to 6 hours on Low settings.
3. Mix well and blend the dip with a hand blender.
4. Serve.

Nutrition Info:
- Info Per Serving: Calories: 244, Total Fat: 11.5g, Fiber: 1g, Total Carbs: 23.65g, Protein: 13g

Chicken Cordon Bleu Dip

Servings: 6
Cooking Time: 1 Hour And 30 Minutes

Ingredients:
- 16 ounces cream cheese
- 2 chicken breasts, baked and shredded
- 1 cup cheddar cheese, shredded
- 1 cup Swiss cheese, shredded
- 3 garlic cloves, minced
- 6 ounces ham, chopped
- 2 tablespoons green onions
- Salt and black pepper to the taste

Directions:
1. In your Crock Pot, mix cream cheese with chicken, cheddar cheese, Swiss cheese, garlic, ham, green onions, salt and pepper, stir, cover and cook on Low for 1 hour and 30 minutes.
2. Divide into bowls and serve as a snack.

Nutrition Info:
- Info calories 243, fat 5, fiber 8, carbs 15, protein 3

Corn Dip

Servings: 2
Cooking Time: 2 Hours

Ingredients:
- 1 cup corn
- 1 tablespoon chives, chopped
- ½ cup heavy cream
- 2 ounces cream cheese, cubed
- ¼ teaspoon chili powder

Directions:
1. In your Crock Pot, mix the corn with the chives and the other ingredients, whisk, put the lid on and cook on Low for 2 hours.
2. Divide into bowls and serve as a dip.

Nutrition Info:
- Info calories 272, fat 5, fiber 10, carbs 12, protein 4

Apple Chutney

Servings: 10
Cooking Time: 9 Hours

Ingredients:
- 1 cup wine vinegar
- 4 oz. brown sugar
- 2 lbs. apples, chopped
- 4 oz. onion, chopped
- 1 jalapeno pepper
- 1 tsp ground cardamom
- ½ tsp ground cinnamon
- 1 tsp chili flakes

Directions:
1. Mix brown sugar with wine vinegar in the Crock Pot.
2. Put the cooker's lid on and set the cooking time to 1 hour on High settings.
3. Add chopped apples and all other ingredients to the cooker.
4. Put the cooker's lid on and set the cooking time to 8 hours on Low settings.
5. Mix well and mash the mixture with a fork.
6. Serve.

Nutrition Info:
- Info Per Serving: Calories: 101, Total Fat: 0.2g, Fiber: 3g, Total Carbs: 25.04g, Protein: 0g

Potato Onion Salsa

Servings: 6
Cooking Time: 8 Hrs

Ingredients:
- 1 sweet onion, chopped
- ¼ cup white vinegar
- 2 tbsp mustard
- Salt and black pepper to the taste
- 1 and ½ lbs. gold potatoes, cut into medium cubes
- ¼ cup dill, chopped
- 1 cup celery, chopped
- Cooking spray

Directions:
1. Grease the base of the Crock Pot with cooking spray.
2. Add onion, potatoes and all other ingredients to the cooker.
3. Put the cooker's lid on and set the cooking time to 8 hours on Low settings.
4. Mix well and serve.

Nutrition Info:
- Info Per Serving: Calories: 251, Total Fat: 6g, Fiber: 7g, Total Carbs: 12g, Protein: 7g

Dill Potato Salad

Servings: 2
Cooking Time: 8 Hours

Ingredients:
- 1 red onion, sliced
- 1 pound gold potatoes, peeled and roughly cubed
- 2 tablespoons balsamic vinegar
- ½ cup heavy cream
- 1 tablespoons mustard
- A pinch of salt and black pepper
- 1 tablespoon dill, chopped
- ½ cup celery, chopped

Directions:
1. In your Crock Pot, mix the potatoes with the cream, mustard and the other ingredients, toss, put the lid on and cook on Low for 8 hours.
2. Divide salad into bowls, and serve as an appetizer.

Nutrition Info:
- Info calories 251, fat 6, fiber 7, carbs 8, protein 7

Crumbly Chickpeas Snack

Servings: 9
Cooking Time: 4 Hrs

Ingredients:
- 1 lb. chickpea, canned, drained
- 4 oz. white onion, peeled and grated
- 1 tbsp minced garlic
- 1 tbsp chili flakes
- ½ tsp thyme
- ½ tsp ground coriander
- 1 tsp salt
- 12 oz. chicken stock
- ½ cup fresh dill, chopped
- 1 tsp butter, melted
- 3 tbsp bread crumbs

Directions:
1. Mix onion with garlic, salt, butter, cinnamon, thyme, and chili flakes.
2. Spread the chickpeas in the Crock Pot and top it with onion mixture.
3. Pour the chicken stock over the chickpeas.
4. Put the cooker's lid on and set the cooking time to 4 hours on High settings.
5. Strain the cooked chickpeas and transfer to the bowl.
6. Top them with breadcrumbs and chopped dill.
7. Serve.

Nutrition Info:
- Info Per Serving: Calories: 270, Total Fat: 5.3g, Fiber: 7g, Total Carbs: 44.09g, Protein: 13g

Tostadas

Servings: 4
Cooking Time: 4 Hours

Ingredients:
- 4 pounds pork shoulder, boneless and cubed
- Salt and black pepper to the taste
- 2 cups coca cola
- 1/3 cup brown sugar
- ½ cup hot sauce
- 2 teaspoons chili powder
- 2 tablespoons tomato paste
- ¼ teaspoon cumin, ground
- 1 cup enchilada sauce
- Corn tortillas, toasted for a few minutes in the oven
- Mexican cheese, shredded for serving
- 4 shredded lettuce leaves, for serving
- Salsa
- Guacamole for serving

Directions:
1. In your Crock Pot, mix 1 cup coke with hot sauce, salsa, sugar, tomato paste, chili powder, cumin and pork, stir, cover and cook on Low for 4 hours.
2. Drain juice from the Crock Pot, transfer meat to a cutting board, shred it, return it to Crock Pot, add the rest of the coke and enchilada sauce and stir.
3. Place tortillas on a working surface, divide pork mix, lettuce leaves, Mexican cheese and guacamole and serve as a snack.

Nutrition Info:
- Info calories 162, fat 3, fiber 6, carbs 12, protein 5

Veggie Spread

Servings: 4
Cooking Time: 7 Hours

Ingredients:
- 1 cup carrots, sliced
- 1 and ½ cups cauliflower florets
- 1/3 cup cashews
- ½ cup turnips, chopped
- 2 and ½ cups water
- 1 cup almond milk
- 1 teaspoon garlic powder
- Salt and black pepper to the taste
- ¼ teaspoon smoked paprika
- ¼ teaspoon mustard powder
- A pinch of salt

Directions:
1. In your Crock Pot, mix carrots with cauliflower, cashews, turnips and water, stir, cover and cook on Low for 7 hours.
2. Drain, transfer to a blender, add almond milk, garlic powder, paprika, mustard powder, salt and pepper, blend well, divide into bowls and serve as a snack.

Nutrition Info:
- Info calories 291, fat 7, fiber 4, carbs 14, protein 3

Lentils Rolls

Servings: 4
Cooking Time: 8 Hours

Ingredients:
- 1 cup brown lentils, cooked
- 1 green cabbage head, leaves separated
- ½ cup onion, chopped
- 1 cup brown rice, already cooked
- 2 ounces white mushrooms, chopped
- ¼ cup pine nuts, toasted
- ¼ cup raisins
- 2 garlic cloves, minced
- 2 tablespoons dill, chopped
- 1 tablespoon olive oil
- 25 ounces marinara sauce
- A pinch of salt and black pepper
- ¼ cup water

Directions:
1. In a bowl, mix lentils with onion, rice, mushrooms, pine nuts, raisins, garlic, dill, salt and pepper and whisk well.
2. Arrange cabbage leaves on a working surface, divide lentils mix and wrap them well.
3. Add marinara sauce and water to your Crock Pot and stir.
4. Add cabbage rolls, cover and cook on Low for 8 hours.
5. Arrange cabbage rolls on a platter and serve.

Nutrition Info:
- Info calories 281, fat 6, fiber 6, carbs 12, protein 3

Turkey Meatballs

Servings: 2
Cooking Time: 7 Hours

Ingredients:
- 1 pound turkey breast, skinless, boneless and ground
- 1 egg, whisked
- 6 ounces canned tomato puree
- 2 tablespoons parsley, chopped
- 1 tablespoon oregano, chopped
- 1 garlic clove, minced
- 1 small yellow onion, chopped
- Salt and black pepper to the taste

Directions:
1. In a bowl, mix the meat with the egg, parsley and the other ingredients except the tomato puree, stir well and shape medium meatballs out of it.
2. Put the meatballs in the Crock Pot, add the tomato puree, put the lid on and cook on Low for 7 hours
3. Arrange the meatballs on a platter and serve as an appetizer.

Nutrition Info:
- Info calories 170, fat 5, fiber 3, carbs 10, protein 7

Potato Cups

Servings: 8
Cooking Time: 8 Hours

Ingredients:
- 5 tbsp mashed potato
- 1 carrot, boiled, cubed
- 3 tbsp green peas
- 1 tsp paprika
- 3 tbsp sour cream
- 1 tsp minced garlic
- 7 oz. puff pastry
- 1 egg yolk, beaten
- 4 oz. Parmesan, shredded

Directions:
1. Mix mashed potato with carrot cubes in a bowl.
2. Stir in sour cream, paprika, green peas, and garlic, then mix well.
3. Spread the puff pastry and slice it into 2x2 inches squares.
4. Place the puff pastry square in the muffin cups of the muffin tray.
5. Press the puff pastry and in the muffin cups and brush it with egg yolk.
6. Divide the potatoes mixture into the muffin cups
7. Place the muffin tray in the Crock Pot.
8. Put the cooker's lid on and set the cooking time to 8 hours on Low settings.
9. Serve.

Nutrition Info:
- Info Per Serving: Calories: 387, Total Fat: 11.5g, Fiber: 6g, Total Carbs: 59.01g, Protein: 13g

Beef, Pork & Lamb Recipes

Beef, Pork & Lamb Recipes

Cinnamon Lamb

Servings: 2
Cooking Time: 6 Hours

Ingredients:
- 1 pound lamb chops
- 1 teaspoon cinnamon powder
- 1 red onion, chopped
- 1 tablespoon avocado oil
- 1 tablespoon oregano, chopped
- ½ cup beef stock
- 1 tablespoon chives, chopped

Directions:
1. In your Crock Pot, mix the lamb chops with the cinnamon and the other ingredients, toss, put the lid on and cook on Low for 6 hours.
2. Divide the chops between plates and serve with a side salad.

Nutrition Info:
- Info calories 253, fat 14, fiber 2, carbs 6, protein 18

Meatballs In Vodka Sauce

Servings:4
Cooking Time: 6 Hours

Ingredients:
- 1-pound ground pork
- 1 onion, diced
- 1 teaspoon ground black pepper
- 1 tablespoon semolina
- 1 cup vodka sauce
- 2 tablespoons sesame oil

Directions:
1. In the mixing bowl mix ground pork with onion, ground black pepper, and semolina.
2. Make the small meatballs.
3. Brush the Crock Pot bottom with sesame oil and put the meatballs inside in one layer.
4. Add vodka sauce and close the lid.
5. Cook the meatballs on low for 6 hours.

Nutrition Info:
- InfoPer Serving: 299 calories, 32.9g protein, 10.3g carbohydrates, 13.4g fat, 0.8g fiber, 85mg cholesterol, 286mg sodium, 529mg potassium

Hot Beef

Servings:4
Cooking Time: 8 Hours

Ingredients:
- 1-pound beef sirloin, chopped
- 2 tablespoons hot sauce
- 1 tablespoon olive oil
- ½ cup of water

Directions:
1. In the shallow bowl mix hot sauce with olive oil.
2. Then mix beef sirloin with hot sauce mixture and leave for 10 minutes to marinate.
3. Put the marinated beef in the Crock Pot.
4. Add water and close the lid.
5. Cook the meal on Low for 8 hours.

Nutrition Info:
- InfoPer Serving: 241 calories, 34.4g protein, 0.1g carbohydrates, 10.6g fat, 0g fiber, 101mg cholesterol, 266mg sodium, 467mg potassium.

Spicy Beef Curry

Servings:6
Cooking Time: 10 Hours

Ingredients:
- 2 ½ pounds beef chuck, cubed
- 1 onion, chopped
- 2 tablespoons curry powder
- 3 cloves of garlic, minced
- ½-inch ginger, grated
- 2 cups coconut milk, unsweetened
- Salt and pepper to taste

Directions:
1. Place all ingredients in the CrockPot.
2. Close the lid and cook on high for 8 hours or on low for 10 hours.

Nutrition Info:
- Info Calories per serving: 455; Carbohydrates:4.5 g; Protein: 41.3g; Fat: 30.2g; Sugar: 0g; Sodium: 729mg; Fiber: 2.6g

Pork Loin And Cauliflower Rice

Servings: 6
Cooking Time: 8 Hours

Ingredients:
- 3 bacon slices, cooked and chopped
- 3 carrots, chopped
- 2 pounds pork loin roast
- 1 rhubarb stalk, chopped
- 2 bay leaves
- ¼ cup red wine vinegar
- 4 garlic cloves, minced
- Salt and black pepper to the taste
- ¼ cup olive oil
- 1 tablespoon garlic powder
- 1 tablespoon Italian seasoning
- 24 ounces cauliflower rice
- 1 teaspoon turmeric powder
- 1 cup beef stock

Directions:
1. In your Crock Pot, mix bacon with carrots, pork, rhubarb, bay leaves, vinegar, salt, pepper, oil, garlic powder, Italian seasoning, stock and turmeric, toss, cover and cook on Low for 7 hours.

2. Add cauliflower rice, cover, cook on Low for 1 more hour, divide between plates and serve.

Nutrition Info:
- Info calories 310, fat 6, fiber 3, carbs 14, protein 10

Sweet Beef

Servings:4
Cooking Time: 5 Hours

Ingredients:
- 1-pound beef roast, sliced
- 1 tablespoon maple syrup
- 2 tablespoons lemon juice
- 1 teaspoon dried oregano
- 1 cup of water

Directions:
1. Mix water with maple syrup, lemon juice, and dried oregano.
2. Then pour the liquid in the Crock Pot.
3. Add beef roast and close the lid.
4. Cook the meal on High for 5 hours.

Nutrition Info:
- InfoPer Serving: 227 calories, 34.5g protein, 3.8g carbohydrates, 7.2g fat, 0.2g fiber, 101mg cholesterol, 78mg sodium, 483mg potassium.

Creamy Beef

Servings: 2
Cooking Time: 6 Hours

Ingredients:
- 1 pound beef stew meat, cubed
- 1 cup heavy cream
- 1 red onion, sliced
- ½ teaspoon turmeric powder
- 2 tablespoons olive oil
- 3 scallions, chopped
- 1 tablespoon chives, chopped
- A pinch of salt and black pepper

Directions:
1. In your Crock Pot, mix the beef with the cream, onion and the other ingredients, toss, put the lid on and cook on Low for 6 hours.
2. Divide everything between plates and serve.

Nutrition Info:
- Info calories 277, fat 14, fiber 3, carbs 7, protein 17

Lamb Chops

Servings:4
Cooking Time: 5 Hours

Ingredients:
- 1 teaspoon ground black pepper
- ½ teaspoon salt
- 1 teaspoon sesame oil
- 4 lamb chops
- 1/3 cup water

Directions:
1. Sprinkle the lamb chops with sesame oil, salt, and ground black pepper.
2. Place the lamb chops in the Crock Pot and add water.
3. Close the lid and cook the meal on High for 5 hours.

Nutrition Info:
- InfoPer Serving: 169 calories, 23.9g protein, 0.3g carbohydrates, 7.4g fat, 0.1g fiber, 77mg cholesterol, 356mg sodium, 292mg potassium.

Beef Casserole

Servings:5
Cooking Time: 7 Hours

Ingredients:
- 7 oz ground beef
- 1 cup Cheddar cheese, shredded
- ½ cup cream
- 1 teaspoon Italian seasonings
- ½ cup broccoli, chopped

Directions:
1. Mix ground beef with Italian seasonings and put in the Crock Pot.
2. Top the meat with broccoli and Cheddar cheese.
3. Then pour the cream over the casserole mixture and close the lid.
4. Cook the casserole on Low for 7 hours.

Nutrition Info:
- InfoPer Serving: 186 calories, 18.1g protein, 1.7g carbohydrates, 11.6g fat, 0.2g fiber, 64mg cholesterol, 178mg sodium, 220mg potassium.

Seasoned Beef

Servings: 6
Cooking Time: 8 Hours

Ingredients:
- 4 pounds beef roast
- 2 cups beef stock
- 2 sweet potatoes, cubed
- 6 carrots, sliced
- 7 celery stalks, chopped
- 1 yellow onion, chopped
- 1 tablespoon onion powder
- 1 tablespoon garlic powder
- 1 tablespoon sweet paprika
- Salt and black pepper to the taste

Directions:
1. In your Crock Pot, beef with stock, sweet potatoes, carrots, celery, onion, onion powder, garlic powder, paprika, salt and pepper, stir, cover, cook on Low for 8 hours, slice roast, divide between plates, drizzle sauce from the Crock Pot all and serve with the veggies on the side.

Nutrition Info:
- Info calories 372, fat 6, fiber 12, carbs 19, protein 11

Tarragon Pork Chops

Servings: 2
Cooking Time: 6 Hours

Ingredients:
- ½ pound pork chops
- ¼ tablespoons olive oil
- 2 garlic clove, minced
- ¼ teaspoon chili powder
- ½ cup beef stock
- ½ teaspoon coriander, ground
- Salt and black pepper to the taste
- ¼ teaspoon mustard powder
- 1 tablespoon tarragon, chopped

Directions:
1. Grease your Crock Pot with the oil and mix the pork chops with the garlic, stock and the other ingredients inside.
2. Toss, put the lid on, cook on Low for 6 hours, divide between plates and serve with a side salad.

Nutrition Info:
- Info calories 453, fat 16, fiber 8, carbs 7, protein 27

Tomatillo Lamb

Servings: 8
Cooking Time: 7 Hrs.

Ingredients:
- 4 tbsp dried rosemary
- 1 cup tomatillos, chopped
- 1 tbsp minced garlic
- 2 oz fresh rosemary
- 1 onion, grated
- 18 oz lamb leg
- 1 tsp salt
- 1 cup cream
- ½ tsp ground black pepper

Directions:
1. Add tomatillos, garlic, dried and fresh rosemary, black pepper, salt, and onion to a blender jug.
2. Blend the tomatillos mixture until smooth.
3. Add lamb leg to the insert of the Crock Pot and pour the tomatillo mixture on top.
4. Put the cooker's lid on and set the cooking time to 7 hours on Low settings.

5. Serve warm.

Nutrition Info:
- Info Per Serving: Calories: 168, Total Fat: 9.8g, Fiber: 2g, Total Carbs: 5.61g, Protein: 14g

Lamb And Zucchini Mix

Servings: 2
Cooking Time: 4 Hours

Ingredients:
- 1 pound lamb stew meat, ground
- 2 zucchinis, cubed
- 2 teaspoons olive oil
- 1 carrot, peeled and sliced
- ½ cup beef stock
- 2 tablespoons tomato paste
- ½ teaspoon cumin, ground
- 1 tablespoon chives, chopped
- A pinch of salt and black pepper

Directions:
1. In your Crock Pot, mix the lamb with the zucchinis, oil, carrot and the other ingredients, toss, put the lid on and cook on High for 4 hours.
2. Divide the mix into bowls and serve hot.

Nutrition Info:
- Info calories 254, fat 14, fiber 3, carbs 6, protein 17

Mustard Ribs

Servings: 2
Cooking Time: 8 Hours

Ingredients:
- 2 beef short ribs, cut into individual ribs
- Salt and black pepper to the taste
- ½ cup ketchup
- 1 tablespoon balsamic vinegar
- 1 tablespoon mustard
- 1 tablespoon chives, chopped

Directions:
1. In your Crock Pot, combine the ribs with the ketchup, salt, pepper and the other ingredients, toss, put the lid on and cook on Low for 8 hours.
2. Divide between plates and serve with a side salad.

Nutrition Info:
- Info calories 284, fat 7, 4, carbs 18, protein 20

Crockpot Beef Stew

Servings: 8
Cooking Time: 10 Hours

Ingredients:
- 1-pound grass-fed beef stew meat, cubed
- 1 onion, chopped
- 1 cup tomatoes, crushed
- 2 cloves of garlic, minced
- 4 sprigs of thyme
- 3 stalks of celery, chopped
- 2 bay leaves
- 2 tablespoons parsley, chopped
- 2 tablespoons apple cider vinegar
- Salt and pepper to taste

Directions:
1. Place all ingredients in the CrockPot.
2. Close the lid and cook on high for 8 hours or on low for 10 hours.

Nutrition Info:
- Info Calories per serving:124; Carbohydrates: 2.1g; Protein: 11.5g; Fat: 8.9g; Sugar: 0g; Sodium: 420mg; Fiber: 0.8g

Lamb Leg With Sweet Potatoes

Servings: 4
Cooking Time: 8 Hrs.

Ingredients:
- 2 tbsp olive oil
- 1 lamb leg, bone-in
- 1 garlic head, peeled and cloves separated
- 5 sweet potatoes, cubed
- 5 rosemary springs
- 2 cups chicken stock
- Salt and black pepper to the taste

Directions:
1. Liberally rub the lamb leg with salt, black pepper, and oil.
2. Place the lamb leg along with other ingredients in the Crock Pot.
3. Put the cooker's lid on and set the cooking time to 8 hours on Low settings.
4. Serve warm.

Nutrition Info:
- Info Per Serving: Calories: 350, Total Fat: 6g, Fiber: 5g, Total Carbs: 12g, Protein: 22g

Aromatic Lamb

Servings: 4
Cooking Time: Hours

Ingredients:
- 1 tablespoon minced garlic
- 1 teaspoon ground black pepper
- ½ teaspoon salt
- 1 teaspoon sesame oil
- 1-pound lamb sirloin, chopped
- ½ cup of water

Directions:
1. Mix the lamb with minced garlic, ground black pepper, and salt.
2. Then sprinkle the meat with sesame oil and transfer in the Crock Pot.
3. Add water and cook the meat on low for 8 hours.

Nutrition Info:
- InfoPer Serving: 246 calories, 32.3g protein, 1g carbohydrates, 11.6g fat, 0.2g fiber, 104mg cholesterol, 373mg sodium, 393mg potassium.

Dessert Recipes

Dessert Recipes

Overnight Plum Pudding

Servings: 8
Cooking Time: 8 1/4 Hours

Ingredients:
- 1 1/2 cups all-purpose flour
- 1/4 cup dark brown sugar
- 1/2 teaspoon baking soda
- 4 tablespoons butter, softened
- 2 eggs
- 1 cup mixed dried fruits, chopped
- 1/2 cup dried plums, chopped
- 1 cup hot water

Directions:
1. Mix the dried fruits, plums and hot water in a bowl and allow to soak up for 10 minutes.
2. Combine the flour, brown sugar, baking soda, butter, eggs and the dried fruits plus the water in a large bowl.
3. Mix well with a spoon or spatula then spoon the batter in your crock pot.
4. Cover and cook on low settings for 8 hours.
5. Allow the pudding to cool in the pot before serving.

S'mores Baked Sweet Potatoes

Servings: 8
Cooking Time: 3 1/2 Hours

Ingredients:
- 2 large sweet potatoes, peeled and diced
- 1 teaspoon cinnamon powder
- 2 tablespoons brown sugar
- 1 1/2 cups crushed graham crackers
- 1/4 cup butter, melted
- 1 1/2 cups dark chocolate chips
- 2 cups mini marshmallows

Directions:
1. Mix the crackers and butter in a bowl. Transfer this mixture in your Crock Pot and press it well on the bottom of the pot.
2. Mix the sweet potatoes with the cinnamon and brown sugar then transfer this mix over the crackers crust.
3. Top the potatoes with chocolate chips, followed by marshmallows.
4. Cook on low settings for 3 hours.
5. Allow the dessert to cool down slightly before serving.

Maple Roasted Pears

Servings: 4
Cooking Time: 6 1/4 Hours

Ingredients:
- 4 ripe pears, carefully peeled and cored
- 1/4 cup maple syrup
- 1/4 cup white wine
- 1/2 cup water
- 1 teaspoon grated ginger
- 1 cinnamon stick
- 2 cardamom pods, crushed

Directions:
1. Combine all the ingredients in your Crock Pot.
2. Cover with a lid and cook on low settings for 6 hours.
3. Allow to cool before serving.

Coconut Vanilla Pudding

Servings: 4
Cooking Time: 1 Hr.

Ingredients:
- 1 and 2/3 cups of coconut milk
- 1 tbsp gelatin
- 6 tbsp sugar
- 3 egg yolks
- ½ tsp vanilla extract

Directions:
1. Whisk gelatin with 1 tbsp coconut milk in a bowl.
2. Transfer this gelatin mixture to the insert of Crock Pot.
3. Stir in milk, egg yolks, sugar, and vanilla.
4. Put the cooker's lid on and set the cooking time to 1 hour on High settings.
5. Serve chilled.

Nutrition Info:
- Info Per Serving: Calories: 170, Total Fat: 2g, Fiber: 0g, Total Carbs: 6g, Protein: 2g

Fudgy Raspberry Chocolate Bread Pudding

Servings: 8
Cooking Time: 6 1/4 Hours

Ingredients:
- 6 cups bread cubes
- 1/4 cup cocoa powder
- 2 cups whole milk
- 1 cup heavy cream
- 1 1/2 cups fresh raspberries
- 1/2 cup white chocolate chips

Directions:
1. Mix the bread cubes, raspberries and white chocolate chips in your Crock Pot.
2. Combine the cocoa powder, milk and cream in a bowl and give it a good mix. Pour this mix over the bread cubes.
3. Cover the pot with its lid and cook on low settings for 6 hours.
4. Allow to cool slightly before serving.

Cream Cheese Brownies

Servings: 12
Cooking Time: 4 1/2 Hours

Ingredients:
- 1 cup dark chocolate chips
- 1/2 cup butter
- 3 eggs
- 1/2 cup sugar
- 1 cup all-purpose flour
- 1/4 teaspoon salt
- 2 cups cream cheese
- 1/4 cup white sugar
- 2 eggs
- 1 teaspoon vanilla extract

Directions:
1. Melt the chocolate chips and butter in a heatproof bowl over a hot water bath. Remove from heat and add the eggs and sugar and mix well.
2. Fold in the flour and salt then pour the batter in your crock pot.
3. For the cream cheese mix, combine the cream cheese, sugar, eggs and vanilla in a bowl.
4. Drop spoonfuls of cream cheese over the chocolate batter and swirl it around with a fork.
5. Cover the pot and cook on low settings for 4 hours.
6. Allow the brownies to cool in the pot before serving.

Pears Jam

Servings: 12
Cooking Time: 3 Hours

Ingredients:
- 8 pears, cored and cut into quarters
- 2 apples, peeled, cored and cut into quarters
- ½ cup apple juice
- 1 teaspoon cinnamon, ground

Directions:
1. In your Crock Pot, mix pears with apples, cinnamon and apple juice, stir, cover and cook on High for 3 hours.
2. Blend using an immersion blender, divide jam into jars and keep in a cold place until you serve it.

Nutrition Info:
- Info calories 100, fat 1, fiber 2, carbs 20, protein 3

Raisin-flax Meal Bars

Servings: 8
Cooking Time: 3.5 Hrs.

Ingredients:
- ¼ cup raisins
- 1 cup oat flour
- 1 egg, whisked
- 4 oz banana, mashed
- 5 oz milk
- 1 tbsp flax meal
- 1 tsp ground cinnamon
- ½ tsp baking soda
- 1 tbsp lemon juice
- 1 tbsp butter
- 1 tbsp flour

Directions:
1. Whisk egg with mashed banana, oat flour, milk, flax meal, raising in a bowl.
2. Stir in cinnamon, lemon juice, baking soda, and flour, then knead well.
3. Grease the insert of the Crock Pot with butter.
4. Make big balls out of this raisin dough and shape them into 3-4 inches bars.
5. Place these bars in the insert of the Crock Pot.
6. Put the cooker's lid on and set the cooking time to 3 hours on Low settings.
7. Serve when chilled.

Nutrition Info:
- Info Per Serving: Calories: 152, Total Fat: 3.7g, Fiber: 2g, Total Carbs: 26.74g, Protein: 4g

Oat Topped Apples

Servings 6
Cooking Time 4 14 Hours

Ingredients:
- 6 Granny Smith apples
- 1 cup golden raisins
- 2 tablespoons brown sugar
- 1 cup rolled oats
- 14 cup all-purpose flour
- 14 cup butter, chilled and cubed
- 12 cup apple cider

Directions:

1. Carefully core the apples and place them in your Crock Pot.
2. Mix the raisins with brown sugar and stuff the apples with this mix.
3. For the topping, combine the oats, flour and butter and mix well until grainy.
4. Spoon the topping over each apple then pour the cider in the pot.
5. Cook on low settings for 4 hours.
6. Serve the apples chilled.

Cinnamon Cream Dessert

Servings: 6
Cooking Time: 1 Hr.

Ingredients:
- 2 cups fresh cream
- 1 tsp cinnamon powder
- 6 egg yolks
- 5 tbsp white sugar
- Zest of 1 orange, grated
- A pinch of nutmeg for serving
- 4 tbsp sugar
- 2 cups of water

Directions:
1. Whisk cream with orange zest, nutmeg, and cinnamon in a bowl.
2. Beat egg yolks with sugar in another.
3. Stir in cream mixture and mix it gently.
4. Divide this cream mixture into the ramekins.
5. Place these ramekins in the insert of Crock Pot then pour 2 cups of water into it.
6. Put the cooker's lid on and set the cooking time to 1 hour on Low settings.
7. Allow it to cool and serve.

Nutrition Info:
- Info Per Serving: Calories: 200, Total Fat: 4g, Fiber: 5g, Total Carbs: 15g, Protein: 5g

Vanilla Crème Cups

Servings: 4
Cooking Time: 3 Hrs.

Ingredients:

- 1 tbsp vanilla extract
- 1 cup of sugar
- ½ cup heavy cream, whipped
- 7 egg yolks, whisked

Directions:

1. Mix egg yolks with sugar, vanilla extract, and cream in a mixer.
2. Pour this creamy mixture into 4 ramekins.
3. Pour 1 cup water into the insert of Crock Pot.
4. Place the ramekins the cooker.
5. Put the cooker's lid on and set the cooking time to 3 hours on Low settings.
6. Serve.

Nutrition Info:

- Info Per Serving: Calories: 254, Total Fat: 13.5g, Fiber: 0g, Total Carbs: 26.84g, Protein: 5g

Blueberry Dumpling Pie

Servings: 8
Cooking Time: 5 1/2 Hours

Ingredients:

- 1 1/2 pounds fresh blueberries
- 2 tablespoons cornstarch
- 1/4 cup light brown sugar
- 1 tablespoon lemon zest
- 1/2 cup butter, chilled and cubed
- 1 1/2 cups all-purpose flour
- 1/2 teaspoon salt
- 1 teaspoon baking powder
- 2 tablespoons white sugar
- 2/3 cup buttermilk, chilled

Directions:

1. Mix the blueberries, cornstarch, brown sugar and lemon zest in your Crock Pot.
2. For the dumpling topping, mix the flour, salt, baking powder, sugar and butter in a bowl and mix until sandy.
3. Stir in the buttermilk and give it a quick mix.
4. Drop spoonfuls of batter over the blueberries and

cook on low settings for 5 hours.
5. Allow the dessert to cool completely before serving.

Hazelnut Crumble Cheesecake

Servings: 8
Cooking Time: 6 1/2 Hours

Ingredients:

- Crust and topping:
- 3/4 cup butter, chilled and cubed
- 1 1/4 cups all-purpose flour
- 1 cup ground hazelnuts
- 1/4 cup buttermilk
- 1 pinch salt
- 2 tablespoons light brown sugar
- Filling:
- 20 oz. cream cheese
- 1/2 cup sour cream
- 1/2 cup white sugar
- 1 teaspoon vanilla extract
- 2 tablespoons Grand Marnier
- 1 tablespoon cornstarch
- 2 eggs

Directions:

1. For the crust and topping, combine all the ingredients in a food processor and pulse until a dough comes together. Cut the dough in half. Wrap one half in plastic wrap and place in the fridge. The remaining dough, roll it into a thin sheet and place it in your Crock Pot, trimming the edges if needed.
2. For the filling, mix all the ingredients in a large bowl. Pour this mixture over the crust.
3. For the topping, remove the dough from the fridge then grate it on a large grater over the cheesecake filling.
4. Cover the pot and bake for 6 hours on low settings.
5. Allow to cool completely before slicing and serving.

Cocoa Peanut Candies

Servings: 11
Cooking Time: 2.5 Hrs.

Ingredients:

- 6 tbsp, peanuts, roasted and crushed
- 8 oz dark chocolate, crushed
- ¼ cup of cocoa powder
- 4 tbsp chocolate chips
- 3 tbsp heavy cream

Directions:

1. Add roasted peanuts and rest of the ingredients to the insert of Crock Pot.
2. Put the cooker's lid on and set the cooking time to 5 hours on Low settings.
3. Divide this chocolate mixture into a silicone candy molds tray.
4. Place this tray in the refrigerator for 2 hours.
5. Serve.

Nutrition Info:

- Info Per Serving: Calories: 229, Total Fat: 15.8g, Fiber: 3g, Total Carbs: 19.02g, Protein: 5g

Strawberry Marmalade

Servings:8
Cooking Time: 4 Hours

Ingredients:

- 2 cups strawberries, chopped
- 1 cup of sugar
- ¼ cup lemon juice
- 2 oz water

Directions:

1. Put all ingredients in the Crock Pot and gently mix.
2. Then close the lid and cook the mixture on low for 4 hours.
3. Transfer the cooked mixture in the silicone molds and leave to cool for up to 8 hours.

Nutrition Info:

- InfoPer Serving: 107 calories, 0.3g protein, 27.9g carbohydrates, 0.2g fat, 0.8g fiber, 0mg cholesterol, 2mg sodium, 65mg potassium.

Apple Cinnamon Brioche Pudding

Servings: 8
Cooking Time: 6 1/2 Hours

Ingredients:

- 16 oz. brioche bread, cubed
- 4 Granny Smith apples, peeled and cubed
- 1 teaspoon cinnamon powder
- 1/2 teaspoon ground ginger
- 2 tablespoons white sugar
- 1 cup evaporated milk
- 1 cup sweetened condensed milk
- 1 cup whole milk
- 4 eggs
- 1 teaspoon vanilla extract

Directions:

1. Mix the brioche bread, apples, cinnamon, ginger and sugar in your crock pot.
2. Combine the three types of milk in a bowl. Add the eggs and vanilla and mix well.
3. Pour this mix over the bread then cover the pot and cook for 6 hours on low settings.
4. The pudding is best served slightly warm.

Cranberries Cream

Servings: 2
Cooking Time: 1 Hour

Ingredients:

- 3 cups cranberries
- ½ cup water
- ½ cup coconut cream
- ½ teaspoon vanilla extract
- ½ teaspoon almond extract
- ½ cup sugar

Directions:

1. In your Crock Pot, mix the cranberries with the water, cream and the other ingredients, whisk, put the lid on and cook on High for 1 hour.
2. Transfer to a blender, pulse well, divide into bowls and serve cold.

Nutrition Info:

- Info calories 100, fat 3, fiber 6, carbs 7, protein 3

BASIC KITCHEN CONVERSIONS & EQUIVALENTS

DRY MEASUREMENTS CONVERSION CHART

3 TEASPOONS = 1 TABLESPOON = 1/16 CUP

6 TEASPOONS = 2 TABLESPOONS = 1/8 CUP

12 TEASPOONS = 4 TABLESPOONS = 1/4 CUP

24 TEASPOONS = 8 TABLESPOONS = 1/2 CUP

36 TEASPOONS = 12 TABLESPOONS = 3/4 CUP

48 TEASPOONS = 16 TABLESPOONS = 1 CUP

METRIC TO US COOKING CONVERSIONS

OVEN TEMPERATURES

120 °C = 250 °F

160 °C = 320 °F

180° C = 350 °F

205 °C = 400 °F

220 °C = 425 °F

LIQUID MEASUREMENTS CONVERSION CHART

8 FLUID OUNCES = 1 CUP = 1/2 PINT = 1/4 QUART

16 FLUID OUNCES = 2 CUPS = 1 PINT = 1/2 QUART

32 FLUID OUNCES = 4 CUPS = 2 PINTS = 1 QUART

= 1/4 GALLON

128 FLUID OUNCES = 16 CUPS = 8 PINTS = 4 QUARTS = 1 GALLON

BAKING IN GRAMS

1 CUP FLOUR = 140 GRAMS

1 CUP SUGAR = 150 GRAMS

1 CUP POWDERED SUGAR = 160 GRAMS

1 CUP HEAVY CREAM = 235 GRAMS

VOLUME

1 MILLILITER = 1/5 TEASPOON

5 ML = 1 TEASPOON

15 ML = 1 TABLESPOON

240 ML = 1 CUP OR 8 FLUID OUNCES

1 LITER = 34 FL. OUNCES

WEIGHT

1 GRAM = .035 OUNCES

100 GRAMS = 3.5 OUNCES

500 GRAMS = 1.1 POUNDS

1 KILOGRAM = 35 OUNCES

US TO METRIC COOKING CONVERSIONS

1/5 TSP = 1 ML

1 TSP = 5 ML

1 TBSP = 15 ML

1 FL OUNCE = 30 ML

1 CUP = 237 ML

1 PINT (2 CUPS) = 473 ML

1 QUART (4 CUPS) = .95 LITER

1 GALLON (16 CUPS) = 3.8 LITERS

1 OZ = 28 GRAMS

1 POUND = 454 GRAMS

BUTTER

1 CUP BUTTER = 2 STICKS = 8 OUNCES = 230 GRAMS = 8 TABLESPOONS

WHAT DOES 1 CUP EQUAL

1 CUP = 8 FLUID OUNCES

1 CUP = 16 TABLESPOONS

1 CUP = 48 TEASPOONS

1 CUP = 1/2 PINT

1 CUP = 1/4 QUART

1 CUP = 1/16 GALLON

1 CUP = 240 ML

BAKING PAN CONVERSIONS

1 CUP ALL-PURPOSE FLOUR = 4.5 OZ

1 CUP ROLLED OATS = 3 OZ 1 LARGE EGG = 1.7 OZ

1 CUP BUTTER = 8 OZ 1 CUP MILK = 8 OZ

1 CUP HEAVY CREAM = 8.4 OZ

1 CUP GRANULATED SUGAR = 7.1 OZ

1 CUP PACKED BROWN SUGAR = 7.75 OZ

1 CUP VEGETABLE OIL = 7.7 OZ

1 CUP UNSIFTED POWDERED SUGAR = 4.4 OZ

BAKING PAN CONVERSIONS

9-INCH ROUND CAKE PAN = 12 CUPS

10-INCH TUBE PAN =16 CUPS

11-INCH BUNDT PAN = 12 CUPS

9-INCH SPRINGFORM PAN = 10 CUPS

9 X 5 INCH LOAF PAN = 8 CUPS

9-INCH SQUARE PAN = 8 CUPS

Slow Cooker
Cookbook

Appendix B : Recipes Index

A

B

C

D

E

F

G

H

I

L

M

T

V

W

Printed in Great Britain
by Amazon